The Complete Alibi Handbook

Mort Weisinger
and Arthur Henley

The Complete
Alibi Handbook

The Citadel Press
Secaucus, N. J.

First edition
Copyright © 1972 by Mort Weisinger and Arthur Henley
All rights reserved
Published by Citadel Press, Inc.
A subsidiary of Lyle Stuart, Inc.
120 Enterprise Ave., Secaucus, N.J. 07094
In Canada: George J. McLeod Limited
73 Bathurst St., Toronto 2B, Ontario
Manufactured in the United States of America
Library of Congress catalog card number: 75-186396
ISBN 0-8065-0264-9

Contents

The Complete Alibi Handbook

Introduction

If you want to survive, you have to be foxy.

This book will show you how to make lies work *for* you when the truth would work *against* you. Face it, friend, you may have to alibi to save face, get out of a jam, get special treatment, be considerate, protect your interests or put someone down. Your alibis can be evasions, disclaimers, buck-passers, softsoap or howls of indignation. But they must be bold, witty and ingenious to be convincing.

Here you will find inspired lies, not just lame excuses. We're not going to give you the tired old cop-outs with which everybody is familiar, clichés like . . .

That was no lady, that was my wife.
The check is in the mail.
I ran into a door.
It happened when I went horseback riding.
My watch stopped.

I took the uptown bus instead of the downtown bus.
I'm glad I'm Jewish.
I had a headache.
That was my twin brother you saw.
I called, but your line was busy.
I got it from sitting on a public toilet.
It wasn't me.

Nobody will be taken in by those old warhorses. You have to be original to stun the cynics in this lying world.

If you think that's being immoral, relax. Great minds know better. Oscar Wilde said: "The one charm of marriage is that it makes a life of deception absolutely necessary for both parties." La Rochefoucauld, the famed philosopher, wrote: "To succeed in the world, we must do everything we can to appear successful." And Dr. Marcel Eck, the French psychiatrist, advises: "Not to speak the truth is sometimes a duty." Even Freud wondered whether "a certain degree of cultural hypocrisy is not indispensable for the maintenance of civilization."

In other words, great minds agree that there are times when alibiing is the civilized thing to do.

The truth can make people uncomfortable. A California politician discovered this when he ran for office on a platform of "honest, straightforward corruption—everything for everybody and a little something for me." So did a New Hampshire politician who proclaimed: "This seeking the position solely for fighting for the people is a lot of hogwash. Personal prestige is the reason why any candidate runs."

P.S.: They lost.

The moral of the story is—lie to win. The wheeler-dealer may be roundly criticized but is secretly respected —if he is successful.

But there's a big difference between lying out of pure meanness and alibiing your way out of a jam. This Ali-bible will show you how to be successful by out-foxing the other guy—or gal.

Caught with the goods

The road to Alibi-ville is paved with good inventions. Your ingenuity is put to the supreme test when you're caught red-handed doing something you shouldn't be doing. Only a clever cop-out can save your reputation and your self-esteem.

Like so:

You've asked your wife to take your suit to the cleaner's. Whenever she does this job for you, she goes through your pockets to make sure they're empty. Shnook that you are, you overlooked one telltale item and she finds it: a slip of paper with seven digits on it. "What's this number—7634858?" she demands.

She'd have to be committed if she didn't guess it was a phone number! Trouble is brewing. How do you cool the confrontation?

A dash of deft deception does the trick. "Oh, I'm glad you found that," you say. "Me and one of my buddies bought a lottery ticket and I jotted down the number so I could watch for it when the winners are published."*

Your hostess hasn't enough closet space so she's asked her female guests to put their coats and handbags in the bedroom. One of the handbags lying there belongs to a gal you suspect of being at least ten years older than she says she is. You can't resist this golden opportunity to sneak a look at her driver's license and learn her real age. But you become so enrapt in your search that you don't hear anyone come in until an angry female voice behind you snaps: "What are you doing going through my handbag?"

Don't debate, just prevaricate: "*Your* handbag! Oh, my goodness, no wonder my glasses aren't here. As you can see, I'm blind as a bat without them!"

Which only goes to show that an "honest mistake" is indistinguishable from a perfect alibi.

---

* Of course, if 7634858 turns out to be a big winner, you'd better take a cram course from Willie Sutton on how to rob a bank.

Anyone who's ever shopped in the local neighborhood has had this happen at least once. Your regular grocery store's biggest competitor, the nearby *A to Z Supermarket*, has a whale of a sale and you can't resist the bargains. You pile your shopping cart high with marked-down items, all those loss leaders that mean money in your pocket. The only way home is to pass your regular grocery store. Just as you go by, the grocer comes out to pick some fruit from his outdoor stalls. He can't possibly miss the big red *A to Z Supermarket* labels on the bags sticking out of your shopping cart. In a plaintive voice, he says, "Sorry to see I lost a good customer."

Bounce right back with this befuddler: "Me do that to you? Never! My baby-sitter is sick so I promised to redeem the poor girl's food stamps. These are *her* groceries."

The grocer will fall all over himself apologizing.

Years ago, you borrowed a book from the local library without using your library card. You shoved it into your bookcase where it still remains. Of course, you've forgotten all about the book until one day your memory is rudely jolted when a visitor happens to pull it off the shelf. Now this visitor happens to be an active member in community projects. When he opens the book, he discovers on the inside cover an official looking sticker that betrays the book as public, not private, property. He gives you an accusing look that clearly means: "You're a crook!"

Alibi time is here. Don't wait for him to say anything. Quickly exclaim: "So *that's* where it was! I misplaced that book years ago and paid the library for it. So anyway it's mine now free and clear."

Now aren't you glad you bought *this* book?

Your husband wants to help you lose weight so he keeps a close watch on your diet. You never realized, though, that he's made a mental inventory of all the delicacies in the refrigerator. So you're caught by surprise when he comes home one afternoon, goes to the refrigerator to pour himself some juice, and exclaims, "Aha! So you went off your diet and ate that whole half a cheesecake that was in the box!"

Cover your tracks with this calorie cop-out. "No, I didn't eat it," you say gloomily. "But I couldn't stand the temptation so I gave it to the cleaning woman."

You're taking a competitive exam for a promotion, twisting and turning to swipe a few answers from other candidate's papers. The proctor catches you and accuses you of cheating.

Time for the Tactical Maneuver Gambit. Cross your fingers and explain: "Look, this exam means a lot to me. I only *acted* like I was cheating so that my competitors wouldn't think I knew the answers and wouldn't copy from *me*."

Attention—all urban cliff-dwellers!

You overlooked a clause in your lease that prohibits tenants from keeping dogs in their apartments. But since you can't bear to part with your pooch, you sneak him out for his daily walks through the basement—until one day the super catches you in the act.

Does this mean "Goodbye, Rover"?

Not necessarily. Just don't try to get away with telling the super you didn't know dogs weren't allowed. That's a weak alibi. Put him on the defensive with this up-to-date deception: "I know what you're thinking, that this is just a dog, right? Wrong! I didn't buy him from a kennel. I bought him from a *security* outfit. He's a real live burglar alarm and my only protection against being robbed!"

These days, even the FBI can't argue with that.

You've hosted a big dinner for some friends and told them your wife made everything herself. After dessert, one of your chums goes into the kitchen to dump his cigar stub in the garbage can. When he raises the lid, he sees exposed a pile of empty frozen food packages—a dead giveaway of the evening meal. "Ha!" he smirks. "So your wife really served frozen food!"

This calls for a shot of anti-truth. Boldly reply: "Certainly not. We were going to serve the frozen stuff but decided to try it out first on the kids. It was just awful, so my wife dug into her recipe file and made the whole meal herself."

You'll be out of the deep-freeze in more ways than one.

You're touring the new imported foods department in the supermarket. A tiny tin of French truffles catches your eye. Three bucks! That's more than you can afford and more than you think it's worth. But since you never tasted truffles, you can't resist sliding the little tin off the shelf and into your shopping bag, rationalizing your larceny by thinking to yourself: "They'll never miss it, and their prices are exorbitant anyway."

You're in for a shock, however, when you turn around and find the store manager eyeing you grimly. He points to your shopping bag and accuses you of shoplifting. This is a serious charge!

What can you do except call your lawyer?

You can act befuddled and bewildered (which you will be, anyway) and mumble: "What? Me shoplifting? Oh, I'm so mixed up since the doctor gave me some new medicine for my bad heart. I just don't know what I'm doing."

No store manager will press charges against a customer who's likely to have a heart attack in his store. But if he asks for the name of your doctor, don't delay in letting the doctor in on your little deception. A bit of collusion goes a long way in making an alibi airtight.

Switcheroo:

You might prefer this way out if you're the aggressive

type. Take the manager by surprise when you're accused and exclaim: "Good for you! I told my consumer group you'd never be fooled. We're conducting a study on how local merchants are dealing with shoplifters, because we know that shoplifting sends prices up. Your alertness will set an example for all the other tradesmen in town. Congratulations!"

You're far from being a pothead but every now and then you join those 15,000,000 Americans whom government agencies say sample marihuana on occasion. So now you're enjoying a quiet evening at home alone, burning a little grass.

The doorbell rings. Nervously, you take a look through the peephole. It's your good neighbor, Sam. No use trying to pretend you're out, because the car's in the driveway and a basketball game's blaring loudly on the TV. Chances are, he wants to watch the game with you.

You have to let him in. So you grind down the butt in an ashtray before opening the door. Sam follows you into the living room, nostrils twitching at the sweet smell that hangs in the air like new-mown hay. It doesn't escape him. "Why, Lew, you old rascal!" he exclaims. "You've been smoking pot!"

Denial is in order, but how?

Here's how. In a shocked voice, retort: "Pot! Are you sure? I've been trying to kick cigarettes and some joker at the office gave me what he called special no-tobacco cigarettes to help me break the habit. He tricked me!"

P.S.: Don't be surprised to learn that good neighbor Sam also smokes "no-tobacco" cigarettes in secret.

You've been putting on weight and have made a sacred vow to your husband that *this* time you'll go on a diet and *stick* to it. Then he walks into the kitchen and catches you nibbling peanuts.

Do you switch to humble pie?

Not if you use the cholesterol cop-out: "Sure I'm eating peanuts *because they're polyunsaturated.* I'm not trying to put on weight, I'm trying to lower my *cholesterol.*"

No health faddist will argue with that kind of logic.

How to checkmate your mate

In the endless strife between husbands and wives, it is sometimes possible to turn a minor disaster into a major victory. For example . . .

Your wife's been pouting all day and you can't imagine why. But when you're ready to turn in, she makes the reason clear. "How come," she asks, "you didn't send me a birthday card?"

Very gently, tell her: "I didn't want to be an old meanie and remind you that you're a year older."

Then douse the light and wish her happy birthday.

Your husband becomes very upset upon receiving a note from the bank advising him that your joint account is overdrawn $100. He surmises—correctly—that you're the culprit.

How will you squirm out?

We have two Dingbat Denials for you, either of which will work. Choose your weapon:

1) "Overdrawn $100? That's impossible, dear. We don't have that much money in the bank."

2) "I was only trying to be considerate because I didn't want you to worry. That's why I didn't enter the checks in the checkbook."

What can you say to a man after you're caught lying to him?

During courtship, you built yourself up to your fiancé by telling him you were a big business exec on a big salary. In fact, you inflated your salary some $2500 per annum.

Well, now you're married. It's income tax time and you're filing a joint return. When your husband sees your withholding form, he says, "Hey, honey, this is wrong. You told me you made $50 more a week than this shows."

Sure you did, in order to catch him. But are you going to tell him now it was a gross exaggeration?

Not if you want to stay married. You need a shameless alibi, and here it is. Deliver it gently: "That's right, dear, but the extra $50 was expenses, not income, so naturally it doesn't show on my withholding form."

He'll regard you as a smart girl for putting him in a lower tax bracket without having to take a loss in "income."

You purchase an expensive vase to give your mother-in-law for her anniversary. On the way to the cashier's, the vase slips out of your hands and breaks into a dozen pieces. Well, you're responsible, so you pay for it, but you know that your husband will hit the ceiling if he finds out.

What can you tell him?

Nothing. Before you leave the store, have the clerk put the pieces neatly into a gift box, wrap it for giving, and package it in brown paper for mailing. Take it to the post office, insure it for twice its value, and send it to your mother-in-law. *Then* tell your husband you sent his mother a lovely vase—period.

When the package arrives, you'll hear from your mother-in-law pronto. Be appropriately surprised and tell her not to be upset, the vase is insured. Give her the insurance receipt—and let her take it from there.

Your mother-in-law will soon have a new vase and your husband will never know what happened.

You think you're pretty foxy when you tell your wife your pay envelope is short $50 because you loaned that amount to your friend, Ben, and he blew it in a poker game. But she's foxier. "Oh yeah?" she says. "Well, I just spoke to Ben's wife. And he told her that *you* borrowed fifty from *him* to win back the fifty you already lost in that same poker game! Now how do you explain that?"

How *do* you?

With this wife-soother: "Well, honey, what else could he tell a distrustful woman like Gladys?"

A woman will believe almost anything if it makes her feel superior to another woman.

You and your wife are dining at a fancy restaurant. While awaiting your main course, the two of you have a bitter argument. Suddenly, she gets up in a huff and walks out on you, just as the waiter comes by bearing two sizzling steaks.

How are you going to explain this humiliation to the curious waiter?

Shield your shame with this shrewdie: "My wife is pregnant. She felt dizzy and ran outside to get some fresh air. She's going to wait for me in the car."

The waiter will be sympathetic and either offer to take back the extra steak or else wrap the two up for you to take home. In any case, you'll have saved face.

You're having a terrific row with your wife, both of you ranting at the top of your lungs. You can't take any more and yank open the door to your apartment, planning to flee to the nearest bar. Before the door slams shut behind you, a pair of ladies' shoes come flying out at you—just as your neighbors are passing through the hall.

There's only one way to save face. Gather up the shoes and yell: "What kind of lifts do you want—rubber or leather?"

By that time the door will have slammed and you can "explain" to the neighbors: "I forgot her shoes. So she tossed them out to me because she isn't dressed."

Same scene. But this row is even louder and is punctuated by the crash of crockery. Again, you duck out, this time safely slamming the door behind you—but almost bumping into the neighbors. They *had* to hear the rumble.

What do you do?

Simply stare at them bewilderedly and ask: "I wonder who in the world was making all that racket."

Then move on, leaving them to puzzle it out.

It's been a miserable evening at home. All through dinner, your wife kept glaring at you, not saying a word. Now that you've plunked yourself in front of the color tube, she snaps off the set and glares again. It's too much. "Dammit!" you explode. "What's got into you? Did I do something wrong?"

She begins to sob. "You know very well what's wrong," she sniffles. "Today's our anniversary and you didn't even send me a card!"

Mister, there is only one way to mend this monumental miscalculation. Act annoyed and disappointed yourself, exclaiming: "Card nothing! You should have received a bottle of perfume from Bloomingdale's* this afternoon. They promised delivery today. Now I'm just as unhappy as you are, sweetheart."

That should get you back in her good graces. Just be sure to bring home a bottle of perfume tomorrow.

The female mind is capable of ingenious alibis. For example . . .

A bill arrives from the department store. It's for clothes you bought yourself. When your husband sees it, he exclaims: "This is ridiculous! Why did you overspend like this?"

Look at him in sheer bewilderment and say: "*Over*spent? I *under*spent! Everything was on sale and I saved you twice as much as I spent. That's being sensible, isn't it?"

No man can withstand that kind of reasoning.

You come home from a shopping spree loaded down with packages. When you tell your husband how much

---

* Substitute the name of a posh department store in your town.

you spent, he roars: "That's almost your whole week's allowance! I thought you promised to stick to your budget."

Don't bat an eyelash. Just say: "Well, with all the burglaries going on, I was afraid to leave any cash at home. And with all the crime going on in the streets, I was afraid to walk around with all that cash on me."

There's no way he can argue back to that.

Drinker's delights

Drinking often presents problems that only a good alibi can resolve . . .

Take the case where you have joined A.A. because you just can't control the booze bit. Now you're at a party where everybody is having a little something except you. Naturally, you don't want to tell anyone the reason why. So when the hostess, in an attempt to be considerate, asks how come you aren't having anything, what do you tell her?

Simply say: "To be perfectly honest, I don't believe in drinking in front of the children . . . and when they aren't around, who needs it?"

Any mother—or father—will savvy that logic.

Here, you're an ultra-respectable community leader, a deacon of your church. So far you've been able to keep your private vices to yourself. But one morning you're seen slipping out of a barroom by a member of the Ladies Aid Society. She gives you a look of disapproval and says: "Before lunch, Mr. Goodenough?"

Smile at her benignly and reply: "I'm having trouble with my digestion and my doctor prescribed a shot of bitters before lunch to soothe my stomach."

That's an old home remedy she'll understand.

You drink too much and your wife is worried that you're becoming an alcoholic. One day she catches you sneaking a belt before lunch and exclaims: "Just as I suspected . . . you *are* an alcoholic!"

Can you convince her otherwise?

Yes, you can. Glass in hand, say to her emphatically: "On the contrary, dear, I have great news! I met a guy who's a doctor and he told me, 'If you want to find out if you're an alcoholic, test yourself by taking a drink when you shouldn't. If you don't want any more, you're not an alcoholic.' Well, honey, I just took the test and passed with flying colors!"

She'll help you celebrate by joining you in a ginger ale on the rocks.

Everyone should be familiar with the standard alibi technique known as the Disclaimer. Its function is to transfer responsibility from yourself to some circumstance beyond your control. Here's an example of how it works . . .

Despite your intention to limit your drinking, you come home one night loaded to the gills. Your wife, plainly fed up, greets you by saying: "Just look at you! What have you got to say for yourself?"

Here's your Disclaimer: "I was overserved."

Try it on your next drunk.

Tailor-made alibis

The authors of this book decided it would be a cop-out on their part if they did not include a select list of able alibis for special people. These are made to order for instant use when the crunch is on.

If you're an Advertising Man . . .

What's your alibi when the boss walks in and finds you stealing a catnap on your office couch?

Leap to your feet, snap your fingers and exclaim excitedly: "Eureka! I've got it! A blockbuster of an idea!"

If you're a Schoolteacher . . .

What's your alibi when a pupil yells to you at the blackboard, "Oh, teacher, you made a mistake!"?

Rebut him with this acid retort: "I was just checking to see if you're awake."

If you're a Portrait Painter . . .

What's your alibi when the subject complains that your painting doesn't look like her?

Salvador Dali says: "It's not important for my portraits to look like the people I paint, but for the people to begin to look like their portraits!"

If you're a Congressman . . .

What's your alibi when a freshman Senator accuses you of lying to that august body?

Debauch him with the D.C. double-talker: "Young man, they know that I'm lying and they know that I know that they know that I'm lying. And that's how we keep each other honest."

If you're a Secretary . . .

What's your alibi when your employer complains he can't read the message you scrawled after taking a phone call?

Deliver this Dingbat Denial: "Well, since I couldn't understand the caller, I didn't write it very clearly."

If you're a Novelist . . .

What's your alibi when you mention another woman's name while making love to your wife?

Flip her this fiction: "It was a Freudian slip, honey. That's the name of the heroine in my next novel."

If you're a Pilot . . .

What's your alibi when your wife demands to know how a technical genius like you could ram the car in front of you on the thruway?

Shoot her this shoptalk: "To tell you the truth, dear, when I started gaining on this other car, I hauled back on the steering wheel, intending to fly over it."

If you're a Draftee . . .

What's your alibi when, after flunking the vision test, you go to the movies and find yourself sitting next to the draft board doctor who examined you?

Give him a nervy nudge with your elbow and inquire: "I beg your pardon, sir, but is this the bus to Poughkeepsie?"

If you're a Baseball Player . . .

What's your alibi when the fans boo you for making an obscene gesture to the crowd?

Flip the fans this face-saver: "I was only pulling on my tender shoulder."

If you're a Gossip Columnist . . .

What's your alibi when people ask you why you

always take your wife along to night clubs when interviewing glamor girls?

Take a tip from columnist Earl Wilson, who says: "I always take my wife along because I'm afraid if I didn't, people might talk—especially my wife."

If you're a Card Sharp . . .

What's your alibi when another player catches you cheating?

Laugh it off with this lulu: "I'll tell you the truth, fellas. I'm taking a course in sleight-of-hand and this game was my test under fire. Who else could I try it on except my good friends?"

If you're a Politician . . .

What's your alibi when you lose an election?

Just remind your critics: "An honest man hasn't got a chance against the machine!"

If you're a Repairman . . .

What's your alibi when a customer complains that your bill is too high?

Commiserate with the customer by copping out: "I have to pay my men more, parts have gone sky high, my rent is up . . . I'm a victim of inflation just like you."

If you're a Playwright . . .

What's your alibi when your play flops?

Act like it was no surprise and say: "Everybody told me I was way ahead of my time. I'll just have to write down to the public from now on."

If you're a TV Producer . . .
What's your alibi when your show is cancelled?
Correct their misconception at once: "It wasn't cancelled. I just had to give it up to spend more time with my family. The damn show kept me so busy my kids hardly knew me!"

Status lies

No greater need hath any man or woman for alibis than the need to preserve one's sense of status—real or imaginary.

In order to move up the ladder socially, you changed your name to something more Waspish. When you bump into an old school chum, how can you explain your name change without sounding like a snob?
Just hand him this story: "It sounds incredible but my wife's maiden name was the same as mine. That meant she couldn't change *her* name unless I changed *mine*—so of course I had to agree!"

Otherwise she'd feel more like your sister than your wife, right? Right.

One sweltering afternoon, a status-conscious acquaintance visits your apartment and notices you have only a small fan to cool the place. "Don't you like air-conditioning?" she asks rather snidely.

Lay it on thick. Tell her: "I'd pay anything for air-conditioning but the wiring here won't handle it—unless I give up my refrigerator. So I've got no choice."

She'll accept that, especially since you emphasized your willingness to pay. Status-seekers always equate *willingness* to pay with *ability* to do so, and that makes the alibi work.

You're having a tough time trying to keep up with the Joneses. Your car is beginning to show its age and this doesn't set well with your status-hungry neighbors. One day the guy next door puts it to you bluntly: "Hey, Phil, when are you gonna trade in that old buggy for a new one?"

Give him a surprised look and reply: "Are you kidding? I just got the bugs out of *this* one! Now that I can enjoy it, I'm not gonna swap it in for a lemon like some other guys on this block."

That'll ring true.

It's a sizzling summer's day, perfect weather for a dip in the new pool you just had built in your backyard. And who comes along wanting to take a dip but your neighbor's obnoxious little brat.

How do you turn the kid down?

Just give him the "facts" by explaining things this way: "Gee, I'd love to let you take a swim, but if I do the insurance company will raise the premium on my liability policy by about $150. Tell your father you can have season swimming privileges if it's worth that much to him."

You can be sure that the old man will keep the kid off your premises after getting that message.

You told everybody you'd applied for membership in the exclusive country club. After bragging how you were a shoo-in, your application is rejected.

What are you going to tell the I-told-you-so-crowd?

Con them with this cavalier cop-out: "When they showed me the list of new members, I changed my mind. That club's going down down down."

The only direction they respect is up up up.

You tell everyone you have a big important job at a TV station. Actually, you work as a salesgirl in the shop downstairs. One day a friend comes in and expresses surprise at seeing you working there, snickering: "Hey, I thought you had a big job in TV?"

Don't dispute him. Devastate him with this alibi: "I do, that's why I'm here. We're preparing some specials on consumer buying habits and I'm gathering material for the program."

That's the stuff that documentaries are made of.

You had to give up your maid because you couldn't give her a raise. Now all your friends are asking: "What happened to Louisa?"

Naturally you don't want to demean your social standing by telling them the truth. You have two alternatives:

1) If you intend to replace Louisa with another maid who'll accept lower wages, a *temporary* alibi will do. Simply say: "I just had to let her go after we caught her stealing."

2) But if you have no intention of hiring a new maid, at any price, you need a *final* kind of alibi. Slip them this sophisticated squelcher: "My doctor made me let her go. My circulation is so poor he ordered me to exercise by doing my own housework." Then pause, and add: "I have to jog an hour, too!"

They'll all be at their doctors' for a check-up in the morning.

You wangled yourself an invitation to the swankiest social event of the season. It's the kind of crowd with which you'd like to mingle on a more regular basis. You keep your nose high in the air, brag with the best of them, and it looks like you've got it made. But when the affair breaks up, one fashionable female after another makes her exit swathed luxuriously in furs. You're the only one wearing a plain cloth coat. There's no doubt in your mind what your hostess is thinking when she gives your coat the once-over with a raised eyebrow.

How can you hang on to your new-found social status?

After thanking her for a lovely evening, look down at your coat and remark: "I always do the opposite of what the weatherman says—but *this* time he *was* right. It's much cooler than I expected."

Your hostess will smile understandingly.

One of the most effective status salvagers is the Pace-Setter alibi technique. Say, for example, that a shortage of funds forced you to settle for an imitation fur coat instead of the real thing. One day a snooty acquaintance sees you in your phony leopard skin, starts to admire it, then feels the material and says, "Oh . . . I thought it was the real thing!"

Are you going to turn red with embarrassment?

Not if you use this Pace-Setter alibi. Very firmly, reply: "You thought I'd buy *real* leopard? Perhaps you haven't heard that all those wonderful wild animals are vanishing from Africa. That's why people like Doris Day, Angie Dickinson, and Mary Tyler Moore have switched to fake furs—to protect the environment."

That's a fact—and the snob knows that these ladies can well afford the best.

The male ego . . .

Any time a man feels that his masculinity is at stake,

he's bound to lie. Generally, he measures masculinity by such yardsticks as physical fitness, virility, financial success, social status, and dominance at home. There are all sorts of ploys you can use when you feel your masculinity is being questioned.

If someone suggests that you look bad, insist: "I never felt better in my life."

If you're scrawny, alibi: "That's the price of having brains."

If you put all your money into renting a fancy apartment but can't afford to furnish it well, just say: "I like simplicity."

If your wife behaves like a shrew in company, tell your men friends: "She likes to show off when we're out. She's quite a different girl at home."

If people kid you for being bald, tell them: "Grass doesn't grow on a busy street."

If your kids are dummies, let everybody know: "I didn't raise my kids to be intellectual snobs."

If you're forced to use credit cards in order to live beyond your means, cover your tracks with: "If you use cash these days, they think you're a nobody."

If your affairs with women wind up to zero, alibi your way out with: "Who's got time for that stuff!"

If you are fired, tell everyone: "I had to get out of that rut."

You decide to give yourself a tonsorial treat at one of those fancy barbershops. No sooner do you settle down in the chair when the manicurist approaches you. You're short of cash, however, and can't afford that luxury.

How do you turn her down without sacrificing status?

Shoo her off with this bold bit: "No, thanks. The last time I had a manicure I developed dermatitis on my fingers and now I'm a skin doctor's delight."

She won't want to touch you with a ten-foot pole.

Do you know how to compose your own Alibiography?

You can quickly build yourself up into a **VIP** in any field. Say, for example, that you want it known that you were an All-American football star. Simply clip a photo from the sports pages showing some unidentified player making the big play or the winning touchdown and say, "That's me, putting across another six points!"

Who can prove you are lying? Nobody!

We know one Alibiographer who has hit a homer for the Yankees, stroked the winning crew at Harvard, parachuted three miles, wrestled underwater with an octopus and climbed Mt. Everest—without ever leaving home! All with an assist from faded published photos, of course.

But you needn't restrict yourself to being a superjock. With a little imagination, you can "make it" in big business, politics or the world of arts and letters. Just comb the newspapers for appropriate photos—you're always the guy (or gal) in the shadows, with your back to the camera, or otherwise indistinguishable and unidentified.

MAKING IT IN THE JET SET

You'll need a cram course in cunning and conning to crash the bistros brightened by the beautiful people. If you lied to your date about what a big man about town you are . . . or to a prospective client about your reputation in the best places . . . or to a filthy-rich acquaintance whose good graces you would like to cultivate . . . here are the instant-status alibis that will open doors to the deluxe dining establishments that cater only to the chic, the famous and the affluent. They will also get you equal treatment.

To get a reservation, have your wife or secretary call and say: "Mr. Rockefeller would like a table for four at six-thirty." If you're asked which Mr. Rockefeller, give one of these initials: N, D, or W. There are other Rockefellers besides Nelson, David, and Winthrop, of course, but a snobbish maître d' will never suspect it.

If you haven't time to phone ahead, go directly up to the maître d', greet him by his first name (*very* important as it allows him to feel he's hobnobbing with his betters) and introduce yourself as the friend of Count, Prince, or Marquis Something-or-other.* This royal name-dropping routine makes a most impressive entrance and almost guarantees you a good table.

To appear well-heeled without being a big spender, know your wines. The red carpet will never be swept from under your feet if you order the most expensive French wine on the *sommelier*'s list—making sure in advance that it is available only in *full* bottles. Order a *half*-bottle, which they won't have, and you've made a grand impression without spending a dime.

Here's another tactic to make you look like Daddy Warbucks. Snap your fingers to summon the *sommelier,* then demand a Chateau Lafite '49, well-chilled. He'll be convinced he's dealing with an epicure. A bottle of this heady stuff will set you back about fifty bucks . . . but, relax, there's only a bottle or two to be had anywhere!

If the *sommelier* seems patently embarrassed, say, "All right, do your best. Select something decent for us from your shabby list."

* If you feel uncomfortable using real names, make up a phony exotic name. It will be just as impressive. For example: Count Charbonnay, Prince Bolchornev, or Marquis de la Tuillieries.

You'll have your guests swimming in awesome admiration at your *savoir-faire*!

Cop-outs in code

An alibi is a kind of code language that enables you to say one thing and mean another. When you become proficient at alibiing, you also become proficient at detecting other people's alibis. In other words, you break the code. Here's a fast and easy lesson on how it works.

In the following examples, (A) is the coded alibi, and (B) is the awful truth . . .

(A) "We had to move from Park Avenue because of the robberies."

(B) "We couldn't afford the rent."

(A) "My doctor made me go to work to keep my mind occupied."

(B) "My husband didn't leave me much insurance and I need the money."

(A) "I don't wear my diamonds any more because I'm afraid to take them out of the vault."

(B) "Even the costume jewelry I'm wearing is borrowed."

(A) "I'll never give up this 1950 Hudson because I love the step-down interior."

(B) "Someday . . . someday . . . maybe we'll be able to buy a new car!"

(A) "I never take the turnpike. Superhighways make me nervous."

(B) "I don't want to pay the toll."

(A) "My son decided to go to medical school in Guatemala to be near his girlfriend. Her father's a big shot in Central America."

(B) "No medical school in this country would take him."

(A) "This rug is an heirloom. It gives the place such a nice lived-in look."

(B) "This damned old rug is threadbare."

(A) "I never go formal. I'm a very basic person."

(B) "I don't own an evening gown."

(A) "Our kids are treating us to this holiday so naturally we're trying hard to keep the cost down."

(B) "We can just about make expenses going tourist class and skipping a few meals here and there."

(A) "The deceased was a simple man who couldn't abide ostentation."

(B) "We want the cheapest funeral available."

When you're late

"Sorry I'm late" is not an alibi; it's an apology. Since almost everyone is late to something at some time or other, here is a supply of alibis for every occasion.

You're late getting back to the office after lunch. Naturally, your boss is waiting for an explanation. This is one you prepared in advance.

You hand him a little toy puzzle, saying, "Boss, I saw this in the window of a store a few blocks away and my kid is crazy about puzzles. I just had to get it for him. But I tried out a dozen before I could find one that would be most fun for him. I sure hope he likes it."

If the boss is even distantly related to a human being,

he'll say "Gee, that was thoughtful," instead of "You're fired."

Here is an unassailable alibi for use when you're late coming to work in the morning.

You go up to your boss, foreman or supervisor, and say sheepishly, "Believe me, I'll never take castor oil again the night before a working day!"

What *can* your superior say? Not a word.

You're late again to meet your husband. And he's fuming. Even worse, you've run out of alibis. All you can do is stammer out a lame excuse. This gets him even angrier and the whole evening is ruined.

Never let yourself get into a spot like that. If you can't stop being late, at least be sure to have a stock of usable alibis to draw upon. Make a mental note of these:

1) "I thought you said the *other* side of the street! I've been walking up and down for half an hour. Didn't you see me?*

2) "I needed to go to the john, dear, and had to go ten blocks out of my way to find one."†

---

* This is the put-him-on-the-defensive gambit. Confuse him so that *he'll* need an alibi.

† You can never go wrong by blaming the natural functions. Weak bladders make good alibis.

3) "I should have taken a cab but didn't want to spend the money. So I had to wait twenty minutes for a bus and then it just crept along."*

4) "You're early, aren't you? Didn't you say one-thirty?"†

5) "You here already? What does your watch say?"‡

6) "You were right about that Mrs. Globglob, dear. I had to bump into her and she can talk, talk, talk! How do you get away from someone like that?"§

You missed the wedding ceremony because you and your wife had a row and it took a while to patch things up between you. When you arrive, you *could* say you had a flat or that you were stuck in traffic. But either of these old hat alibis would impress the wedding party only as a

---

* The money angle. With this kind of alibi, you establish your sense of thrift—it's *his* money you're saving.

† No, he said one o'clock, as you know darned well. But if he begins to doubt *himself*, he won't doubt *you*.

‡ Now it's the fault of your watch itself. Naturally, you made sure to turn it back a half-hour or so.

§ Since he's already confessed that he can't get away from Mrs. Globglob, how can you? He made your alibi possible. This is always a good ploy—to take the cue from the other fellow.

lame excuse—even if it was true. You have to come up with a richer, riper ruse that won't be suspect.

Here are some 100-proof gems you can trust:

1) "Our headlights conked out on the parkway and we had to crawl along, using our parking lights, until we got to a service station."*

2 "The radiator boiled over and there was nothing we could do but pull up on the shoulder and wait for it to cool down."†

3) "We ran into an interminable American Legion parade and no cars were allowed through until the whole parade passed by."‡

4) "There was a jack-knifed trailer blocking the highway and we had to wait until a tow truck came and cleared the road."§

5) "We tried to beat the traffic by taking shortcuts. We must have hit half-a-dozen railroad crossings, and at

---

* Good for a dark night.
† Perfect on a hot summer's day.
‡ Ideal on a holiday, or almost any weekend.
§ A natural during commuter's hours.

every one we found a mile-long freight train crawling by."*

Occupational hazards provide grist for the alibi mill. If you neglected to phone your wife not to wait dinner for you, smooth her ruffled feathers when you arrive with one of these smoothies:

"Sorry, dear, but the meeting ran late."

"My luck, a good customer had to come in at closing time!"

"I had to stick around to meet our out-of-town buyer."

"The boss made me hang around to help him give a little send-off to an old-timer who's retiring."†

"There was a power failure in the building. I got trapped in the elevator for an hour—and without an air-conditioner!"

A word of caution . . .

With some people, no matter how much you document, embellish, and establish your alibi, it doesn't work the way it should. Take the case of clever Clyde, whose

---

* Nice all-weather alibi.

† This is especially effective if you stopped off at the tavern and there's booze on your breath.

wife was an absolute nut about punctuality. It was a capital crime to keep her waiting, especially on a street corner. Well, Clyde knew he was going to be late so he prepared an elaborate alibi. He tore his coat, crushed his hat and covered himself with grime. When he met his wife, he told her, panting, "I got caught on the door handle of a taxi and was dragged two blocks before a mounted policeman made a grab for me from his horse!"

Unimpressed, his wife asked, "And that took ten minutes?"

Sometimes too much is still not enough. You have to know who you're talking to.

The dating game

You're riding high in the dating game, with a juicy list of juicy gals in your little black book. You have a date with one of the best for Friday night. But you just met a new number who's even better stuff, and the only free night she has is Friday. You'd like to break your date with Girl #1 without losing her friendship. This poses a problem because she's not the type to take a stand-up gracefully. If she thinks she's been stood up, you're on her "drop dead" list.

How can you manage the difficulty?

Gull the gal with this gambit. Call her on *Thursday* night and say: "I'm so anxious to see you, honey, I wonder if I can pick you up a half-hour earlier tonight?"

She'll be shocked and think she goofed, that she really made the date for Thursday. If she's free, she'll tell you to come over. If not, you can make it for the following week.

This is a classic example of having your cake and eating it.

You've lied to your boyfriend about your age. When you agree to vacation abroad with him, he gets a look at your passport and sees your real age. Clearly miffed, he pouts, "Why did you lie to me about your age?"

Time for a cagey cop-out. Say to him, "Sshhh, sweetie, I didn't lie to you. I lied to *them*. Don't repeat this to anyone, but I had my birth certificate altered years ago so I could come into my trust before I reached maturity."

He'll love you even more because he'll think you're loaded.

Your date takes you to a party to meet some of his crowd. The conversation turns to contemporary adult fiction. One modern novel after another is mentioned. You haven't read any of them and are left out of the conversation. Finally, your embarrassed date takes you aside and says, "Gosh, don't you do *any* reading?"

How can you avoid appearing like an illiterate?

Turn on the sex-appeal and murmur: "Darling, where would a popular girl like me ever find time to *read?*

That should win back his admiration.

You want to date your girlfriend's girlfriend on the q.t. but she has her phone number. How can you get the number and the date without tipping your hand?

Take these six sneaky steps . . .

1) Tell Girl #1 you want Girl #2's phone number for a friend.

2) Ask your friend to phone Girl #2 for a date, using Girl #1 as a reference.

3) At the last minute, have your friend call to say he can't make it—but he knows a great guy (YOU) who can.

4) *You* keep the date.

5) Next day, tell Girl #1 what happened—explaining how you were "stuck" with *her* friend because *your* friend couldn't make it.

6) Be a full-time two-timer by dating both while telling each one separately: "Your friend's okay but you're more fun and prettier."

P.S.: Sooner or later, of course, you're going to have to make a choice—or look for Girl #3!

How do you turn off . . .

A guy who's wined and dined you, takes you home by taxi, then wants to come in to exact his pound of flesh?

Repulse him with this riposte: "Sorry, darling, but my aunt from Reading is visiting me for the weekend."

A dame who insists on a cab, not knowing you're so broke you can just about make bus fare?

Play it big: "Sorry, baby, but I don't have anything smaller than a C-note and some small change. And cabbies won't take any bill over a fiver."

If she offers to lend you the cash, take it.

A guy who keeps pestering you for a dance at a swinging party but whom you want no part of?

Drop this bomb: "You're too nice a guy for me to let you take that chance. My boyfriend is a professional bouncer and will be here soon."

A dame who won't let you alone at a party even after you've told her you're married?

Shock her with this shameless lie: "Incidentally, my wife's name is Charles. You'll have to meet him one day."

She won't bug you after that.

Sometimes you can answer a sticky question with another question to get yourself off the hook. This goes back to the old joke where one person asks another:

"Why do you always answer a question with a question?"
And the other person replies: "Why not?"

It works with alibis, too. Here, for example, you're in
a very intimate embrace with the girl of your momentary
choice. Out of nowhere (or so it seems to you), she asks,
"Do you love me?"

Of course you don't (except momentarily). But this
girl needs some reassurance (not too much). You can't
go wrong if you answer with a question. Take your
choice:

    a) "Do I act like only a casual acquaintance?"

    b) "Do I love you? What do *you* think?"

    c) "If I didn't love you, would I take these liberties?"

    d) "What a question. Could anybody love you more?"

    e) "Don't I always want you?"

If you can't even think of a question, just smile hap-
pily and go on with what you're doing. In this sort of situation, the emotional climate is right for even the weakest
alibi to work successfully.

You're a big man on campus, with a string of girl-
friends at colleges for miles around. To *keep* them on a
string, you stuff their mail boxes with torrid love letters.
One day you discover that you made a horrible goof
—you mixed up two envelopes and sent Dolores' letter to
Cheryl, and vice-versa!

What are you going to do, Mr. Two-Timer, when the
axe falls?

When the great confrontation comes, simply give

Dolores and Cheryl, individually of course, the same story: "Baby, now I can tell you. It was all part of my fraternity initiation. The boys dared me to write you, addressing you by another name, to make you think I was unfaithful. But stunt or no stunt, I meant every word I wrote—and you know I meant it for you alone."

She'll give you that boys-will-be-boys laugh and all will be forgiven.

You and your girlfriend are husband-hunting together at a resort hotel. The two of you agreed in advance that you wouldn't split up; you'd double-date or nothing. But you meet a guy who hasn't got a friend for your friend, and you want to sneak off with him.

How can you get away with it?

Hand your girlfriend this story, very confidentially: "Listen, Jane, this guy is married and I know his wife . . . but *he* doesn't know that I know her! If you want to have a good laugh, I'll give him the business tonight and tell you all about it later."

Five will get you ten that she'll giggle with anticipation at having the horselaugh at his expense—and give you the green light to go ahead.

A handy way out of an awkward situation is the putting-words-in-her-mouth alibi. The idea is to attribute to the other person a remark she *didn't* make—but that sounds like she *might* have made. Once she begins to doubt herself, you've got the edge on her.

Here's an example. Jeff, your girlfriend's beau, asks you out. You accept the date without intending to tell your g.f. about it. But she finds out and confronts you, saying: "What's the big idea of going out with Jeff behind my back?"

There's only one way to deal with this situation. Act very surprised and say: "What do you mean—behind your back? Remember you said to me last week, 'When I'm through with Jeff, you can have him'? So when he asked me out, I went."

She never did say that, of course, but she'll think she *might* have. After all, she and Jeff aren't going steady. The only retort she can make is, "Well, if I did say that, it was only a joke."

Since it's her joke, you're in the clear.*

You fancy yourself as quite a man about town. You do have a pretty good line and do occasionally make out with a classy chick. You have just made such a score and are relaxing now beside the object of your affections. You're feeling quite pleased with yourself, like an in-like-Flynn master, and your smugness obviously shows. The young lady, feeling that she's been had, decides to take you down a few pegs. Scornfully, she snaps, "You're no big deal as a lover!"

---

* Unless she follows it up with this trap: "But I didn't say I was through with him, did I?"

Don't bat an eyelash. Just say coolly: "No, but since he called me up, I figured that was the same thing."

You're back in the clear but good!

That hurts, true or not, and your male instincts rebel.

"Try me again, baby," you snap back, "on a day when I haven't made a big donation to the Artificial Insemination sperm bank!"

Now that was an unfortunate alibi. For the sake of a put-down to preserve your pride and potency, you lied and lost the girl. What you *should* have said is, "Well, baby, with a super-dish like you, a guy's gotta be a superman!"

Flattery will get you seconds.

As the famous lover, Casanova, once remarked: "The man who knows how to alibi will never be caught with his pants down—unless he's in the john or the boudoir."

Whoppers for snoopers

You've been snooping through someone's mail when that someone walks in. You're caught redhanded.

But not dumbfounded. We have a made-to-order alibi for such occasions. Tell it with a smile: "My kid's a nut about stamp collecting and I'm always on the lookout for unusual specimens."

If you get a quizzical look, sock it to 'em harder by adding: "If you come across any goodies, let me have them for the kid, will you?"

This alibi should get a stamp of approval.

A business associate sees you coming out of police headquarters and naturally wonders what's up. The fact of the matter is that your son was picked up on a charge of smoking grass and you went over to arrange bail. But you aren't going to tell this to your curious friend.

What *are* you going to tell him?

Befuddle him with this bit of bunkum: "I happened to be a witness to a hold-up the other night! So the cops called me to come down to headquarters to see if I could identify a suspect in the line-up. It's a civic duty, right?"

The guy will admire your guts—but we admire your gall.

You're doing the voyeur bit—peeping with binoculars through your window at the penthouse patio across the street. There in full focus is a stunning babe sunning herself in all the best places. You're enrapt. It's no time for your mother-in-law to surprise you, exclaiming, "I never would've believed it—you're a Peeping Tom!"

Nu?

Act surprised yourself (which you will be) and protest, "Of course not, mom. My car is parked downstairs and I was just looking to see if my time is up on the meter."

If you do this with finesse, she may even offer to lend you a dime.

You're exchanging gossip with another woman and pass along the word that a mutual acquaintance's husband is suspected of cheating. Well, you told the wrong person because later that afternoon the wife in question telephones and says icily, "I hear you've seen my husband with another woman. I want the facts!"

There's only one thing to do: deny it by using the T.T.R.* alibi. Say to her, "Don't believe everything you hear. If I saw him, I wouldn't look. If I looked, I wouldn't recognize him. And if I recognized him, I wouldn't remember. So what's there to tell you?"

Before she can recover, change the subject.

How to fend off *Nosy Questions* . . .

When people pry into your personal affairs, protect your privacy with a potent prevarication. Take this typical nosy question: *"How old are you?"*

Don't answer directly. Use one of these squelchers:

"I feel like 105."

"Neither as old as you think nor as young as I look."

"Well, I get into *X*-rated movies by myself."

"A year older than last year."

"If you can't tell, I must look older than I feel."

"You'll never guess."

There are times when Mr. or Mrs. Nosybody must be put down with a *euphemism*—a socially acceptable word or phrase that serves to conceal a less socially acceptable

* Topsy Turvy Reasoning.

situation. Here is a typical question that is best dealt with by euphemisms: *"What does your husband do?"*

If his occupation isn't something you want to brag about, use a euphemism to conceal it:

"He has his own business." (A candy store)

"He's in the construction business." (A laborer)

"He's on Wall Street." (A messenger)

"He's in banking." (A teller)

"He's in the food line." (A supermarket clerk)

"He works for the government." (A mail carrier)

"He's a railroad man." (A conductor)

"He's in merchandising." (A door-to-door salesman)

"He's retired." (On Social Security)

The result is instant status!

Never underestimate the power of the little word *So*. When you answer one question with another question, your alibi tends to sound more logical, obvious and convincing if it starts off with "So . . ."

Let's say that someone asks you: *"Why didn't you get the raise?"*

You needn't go into long explanations.* Just slip 'em any one of these squelchers:

"So the government can take it?"

"So my wife could go to the beauty parlor *twice* a week?

---

* If you go on the defensive, whatever you say will sound like sour grapes. But the "So . . ." alibis give the impression that you *refused* the raise.

"So my relatives will think I'm rich and sponge off me?"

"So I should work even harder for that Simon Legree?"

To tell the truth

Remember that an alibi can be a perfectly legitimate excuse. It needn't be a lie at all. In fact, there are times when the absolute *truth*—if blurted out unexpectedly—can be positively convincing.

When heavyweight champ Jack Dempsey was knocked down by Gene Tunney, he copped out with this humble mumble: "I forgot to duck."

Let's say you live in a modest apartment that doesn't reflect the high rent you pay. A snobbish friend comes in, looks around, and comments: "A person like you should live in a more expensive apartment."

Don't crawl into a hole. Tell him the *truth*: "I'm going to. Next month my landlord is raising my rent."

Your visitor will chuckle and realize you aren't as insolvent as you seem to be.

There are many situations where the truth may be your best alibi because it is so outrageous that it simply cannot be believed. Suppose, for example, that you're a married man who bumped into an old girl friend and spent the night with her. You tiptoe into your house at dawn and are startled to discover your wife awake.

Beat her to the punch before she can say a word. Very sincerely, say, "Honey, I'm going to tell you the truth and throw myself upon your mercy. I had a drink at this bar after work and met this gorgeous dame. We got to talking and she invited me to her duplex where we had a few more drinks. Then she made dinner for me and told me she was a divorcée and very lonely. She said I was her type of man and became very romantic. Then she threw herself at me and I just couldn't resist. She was drunk with passion and I couldn't get away until now."

After this straight-from-the-shoulder recitation, your wife will stop the filibuster with: "You're drunk yourself. Why don't you stop lying and just admit you were playing poker with the boys all night?"

Here's another example. You're called to jury duty but don't want to serve for fear of losing your job. You're worried that your boss will never miss you and decide he can do without you. But you offer instead a weak alibi, telling the court clerk, "I just can't take time off from my job."

The clerk is bound to reply, "You must be one of those people who thinks your boss can't get along without you, eh?"

Now tell him the truth: "No, but I don't want him to find it out!"

Sometimes, though, you can't be truthful even when your excuse is perfectly legitimate. This happens when an excuse, no matter how true, has been overworked to the point of becoming a cliché, hence unbelievable.

For example, take a case where you're late to work. Actually, it wasn't your fault. You started out early enough but the thruway was jammed and you got stuck in a bumper-to-bumper bottleneck. If you told that to your boss, he'd scoff, "Don't hand me that old chestnut!"

More believable will be a finely fabricated alibi like this: "Boss, you may not believe this, but*—what happened was I took my Chevvy in to the car laundry and it got trapped there for an hour when their conveyor belt got stuck. That's what held me up."

And that he *will* believe.

If you want to make it socially, you'd better master the art of the evasive alibi. You don't tell the truth, but you don't lie either. You simply skirt the issue by delivering a *No-Lie Lie*. Here's an example of how it works . . .

Your mother-in-law drops in to show off her new spring suit. Clearly expecting a compliment, she asks, "What do you think of it?"

---

* The phrase—*you may not believe this, but*—is called a *Handle*. It insures your alibi by setting the groundwork for belief when your copout sounds too incredible to be accepted at face value. Here are some other Handles that imply you're taking your listener into your confidence:

"Don't mention this to anyone, but . . ."
"I didn't mean to tell you this, but . . ."
"Promise you won't tell anyone, but . . ."

You smile approvingly: "That suit is really *you!*"

To someone expecting a compliment, that *is* a compliment.

Even if she looks as if she robbed a scarecrow, here are other No-Lie Lies that will sound complimentary:

"It's really something."*

"What a buy!†

"It's made beautifully."‡

"What gorgeous material!"§

"Fantastic!"**

You never once said the suit looked well on her—but neither did you say it didn't.

The No-Lie Lie can save your husband's job . . .

Consider the problem of how not to offend his boss' wife. The old girl is approaching middle age but seems to be approaching it from the wrong direction. Looking to you for reassurance, she asks, "I don't look 40, do I?"

You'd just love to be bitchy enough to reply, "No, dear, not any more!" But of course you're too smart to do anything so foolish. You merely reply: "You certainly don't."

---

* So is a gunny sack.

† That puts it on a money basis, making her feel like a wise shopper.

‡ Even though it doesn't fit well.

§ But, oh, what's inside!

** Translation: an unbelievable sight.

That makes the truth and the lie inseparable—and indistinguishable.

The No-Lie Lie can save a friendship . . .

Take the case where you're a wedding guest. Naturally, you're expected to say something nice about the bride, who is hideous.

You needn't lie. Just use one of these ambiguous alibis:

"That's what I call a real bride."

"She certainly has grown up!"

"I can't wait to see her bridal photographs."

"She never looked more beautiful."

Every comment will be interpreted as a lavish compliment.

The noncommittal comment is a great convincer because it plays upon your listener's vanity. All you have to do is pile on the praise minus the particulars. Here's a crash course in alibiing that demonstrates how it's done—one No-Lie Lie after another . . .

A friend of yours who yearns to be an actress finally gets a part in a television play. As soon as the telecast is over, she calls you up. It's pretty embarrassing because you completely forgot to watch the show!

Forget about being embarrassed. Here are the questions she'll probably ask, and the alibis (*in italics*) guaranteed to get you off the hook:

"Did you catch the show?"

"Did I!"

"Oh, great. How did you like my performance?"

"You were everything I expected you would be."

"Thank you so much. Which scene did you like best?"

"To tell you the truth, I liked them all."

"I'm so glad. Tell me, do you think I have as much talent as Mary Tyler Moore?"

"Sweetie, even Mary Tyler Moore doesn't have what you have."

"You're a real darling and I love you."

Give yourself an "A" for the course.

Dodging your creditors and getting your money's worth

In these days of inflation and recession, you have to be among the Rich and the Super-Rich to meet your bills on time. When you're hard up for cash, here are some *Artful Dodges* that will keep your credit rating intact and hold off your creditors until there's money in the bank.

1) Ignore all bills until you receive a threatening letter.

2) Return that part of your statement that identifies you—but "forget" to enclose a check.

3) Or—enclose the *wrong* check, made out to another company.

4) Or—*don't sign* the check.

5) Or—just pay *part* of the bill.

6) Return the entire statement with a note that says: "Are you sure this is accurate?"

7) Disregard the bill completely as though you'd never received it, and send a letter saying: "I believe I owe you money. Would you please send an itemized bill?"

8) Answer all dunning letters with this memo: "Check was mailed on *(insert a date of a week or more ago)*. If not received in two weeks, please let me know."

9) If your creditor calls you on the telephone, and the bill is *small* (under $50), say: "Send me a letter when you want to go to court." They won't sue for a small amount and you'll have time to raise the money. If the bill is *large*, say: "I'm going to have to declare bankruptcy if you press me, and then you won't get a cent." They'll wait.

P.S. *(to Bold Bluffers):* If you've let the bills pile up unanswered and your credit rating is being threatened, it is time to pay up. But you can reinstate your good credit rating by denying ever having received the bills in the first place.* Blame the Post Office, or suggest they might

* Remember—you are not legally responsible for either receiving or opening your mail. The onus is on the sender.

have been thrown out with the junk mail, or say they were in your mailbox—unopened—because you were away (in the hospital, on a business trip, or on vacation).

How do you alibi to the computer colossus?

Here's a book club that's been bugging you to pay up. The truth of the matter, however, is that you had ordered a book, read it from cover to cover the day you received it, and didn't like it. To avoid having to pay for it, you repacked it in its original box, re-sealed it, and marked the package: "Refused—Return to Sender." But the computer never noticed. You've been billed three times for the book and you keep sending back letters, lying that you never accepted the book. Now, in the envelope with news about the book club's latest selection, you find a bill marked: FINAL NOTICE.

Don't panic. Just take the enclosed return card on which you're supposed to indicate whether you want the current selection or a substitute and write down this substitute "title": *Final Notice*.

We guarantee that you'll get past the computer and receive a puzzled reply. That will give you a chance to explain the misbilling to a real live human being and have your alibi accepted.

When you need money, you may need an alibi to get it. For example . . .

You're desperately trying to negotiate a loan with a finance company. It seems hopeless. The lender calls you a bad credit risk.

Overpower him with the T.T.R.*: "How can you say that? I owe Macy's $50, my doctor $100, and my landlord 2 months' rent—can *you* get such good credit?"

After that, add the loan shark to your list.

Or take this situation . . .

You're signing up for a loan at the bank when a business acquaintance spots you. "Hard times got you too, eh, Joe?" he asks.

Time for the squelcher. "Not me," you shoot back. "I just never use my own funds for investment purposes."

The next thing you know, he'll be trying to pump you for the secret of your financial success.

Well, your check bounced. It could happen to anyone, but no such luck—it had to happen to you. Now along comes the victim waving the bum check in your face.

There's only one thing to do—beat him to the punch before he gets a chance to say anything. As soon as you see him approaching, start shaking your head sadly, "I know, I know, you're not the only one. I had four other bounces. And shall I tell you the ridiculous reason why? Because a rival bank was offering free gifts to anyone

* Topsy Turvy Reasoning.

who opened a new savings account. My wife had to have a new hair dryer so she dipped into our joint checking account, practically emptied it, got the dryer, and forgot to tell me about it. Oh, women!"

This should get you through. Your check should also go through when the victim redeposits it. A second bounce is not a happy thing to contemplate, even for a Grand Master of the Alibi.

It's the happiest day of the week—pay day. You pick up your pay envelope, look inside and discover that your paycheck is a dollar short. Highly indignant, you stride up to the cashier and register your complaint. She checks the records and says, "You know, last week we overpaid you a dollar. But you didn't complain about the mistake then, did you?"

Without wincing or weaseling, say simply: "An occasional mistake I can overlook—but not two in a row."

A member of the United Mine Workers actually pulled this cop-out to the delight and envy of his co-workers.

There are times when you really don't need an alibi but feel more comfortable using one. For example . . .

You're anxious to save a buck like anybody else these days, and so you've cut down on dining out. But you discover a new restaurant that offers a tremendous deal on a lobster dinner and decide to treat your wife to a night out. You know that the only way this place can afford to keep food prices down is to make it up on drinks. That's what you have to avoid—ordering drinks.

Well, you really don't have to make excuses . . . unless you're the type who feels self-conscious about such things and has to justify your not ordering cocktails. If this is you, don't tell the waiter you and your wife are on the wagon because you have an ulcer or are on a diet. He'll only snicker. Instead, use the *Sotto Voce Stratagem.* As soon as you walk in, take the waiter aside and tell him *sotto voce:* "Listen, my wife's a member of A.A. Please don't even bring a wine list."

He'll nod understandingly and tell you to enjoy your lobster.

Alibis can save you money . . .

You've been dickering with a caterer about a big affair you're planning. The deal's just about signed and sealed when you learn of another caterer who'll give you the same deal a whole lot cheaper.

How do you call off negotiations without risking either an unpleasant scene or a lawsuit?

Just pitch this sad story: "I'm awful sorry but I can't hire the hall. I just found out my guest of honor is strictly kosher."

This leaves him only two alternatives: conversion or capitulation. Naturally, he'll capitulate.

A young man comes to your door and says he's selling

magazines to work his way through college. You don't want to buy any subscriptions at his high prices but you hate to offend the kid.

You needn't offend him. Just alibi: "I hate to turn you down but my husband* is in the advertising business and we get all our magazines free. In fact, we get so many we donate most of them to the local hospitals."

You take your girl to dinner at a big new restaurant that's trying to build up a following. Their promotional gimmick is a coupon in the newspaper that can be exchanged for one free dinner for a party of two. After you've stuffed yourselves, the waiter hands you the check. You hand him cash enough to pay for one dinner plus the coupon. He hands it back, saying: "Sorry, sir, but this offer has expired." You never noticed!

You're in a jam because you're short of cash and this place doesn't honor your credit card. Well, just remember that any promotion-minded bistro is anxious to make a good impression. With this in mind, ask for the manager and tell him: "Look, I forgot to turn this in last week and paid cash for my party. I called later and spoke to someone who said, 'Don't worry about it, just bring it in next time you're here.' Well, this is *next* time."

The manager will honor it to keep a customer.

Somebody phones you for a donation to a big impor-

---

* Any relative will serve the purpose.

tant charity. You already gave at the office but nobody will buy that even if it's true.

How do you squirm out without sounding like Scrooge?

Simple. Go the caller one better with this gasser: "That's a very worthy cause and I respect you going to bat for it. But I have a favorite charity that doesn't get much attention. It's the (*mention some obscure charity*).* If you contribute to *my* charity, I'll match it with a donation to yours. Isn't that fair?"

Absolutely fair—and absolutely safe. We've tested it and it always works because 99 out of 100 times the caller is a professional fund-raiser—in no mood to give, only to be given.

What if you're asked to help out as a volunteer and go from door to door for cash contributions?

Here are some blameless, shameless alibis to get you off:

1) "I'd like to but I'm a Gemini. Nobody would give me anything but a hard time."

2) "I would if I didn't have these palpitations that bother me every time I meet a stranger."

* Here are some worthwhile but less familiar charities you can use: Myasthenia Gravis Foundation, Save the Children Federation, Muscular Dystrophy Association, Children's Asthma Research Institute, National Multiple Sclerosis Society, and National Hemophilia Foundation.

3) "It's a great cause but I'm already committed to another charity."*

Just what the doctor ordered

A psychiatrist says he'll treat you for an hour a week, and that his fee for the hour is $50. Well, this is too rich for your blood. But don't let your neurosis get the better of you.

Tell him, "Listen, Doc, I can't get an hour off from work. Make it a half-hour and I'll talk twice as fast."

This is known as the psychiatric psquelcher.

A nerve specialist charges $20 for the first visit and $10 after that. Figuring to outsmart him, you come in saying, "Hi, Doc, here I am again!"

But he isn't called a nerve specialist for nothing. For after the examination, when you ask what treatment he recommends, he replies, "Just keep on with the same treatment I gave you last time."

The name of the game is Alibi and Counter-Alibi.

* Mention one of the charities listed above.

Your Park Avenue internist hands you a bill for a house visit. "Wow, this is high," you remark. "I can't afford it."

"Then you shouldn't have called in a high-class doctor like me," he replies. "Why didn't you go to a clinic?"

"Because," you tell him, "when it comes to my health, money is no object!"

If he won't swallow that alibi, tell him it makes as much sense as his bill. He'll settle.

The surgeon who removed your gallbladder many stones ago sends you a bill on which he's made the notation: "Tomorrow this bill will be one year old."

Immediately, send back a memo: "Happy birthday!"

Know how to get a doctor to make a house call?

It's practically impossible unlesss you lure him over with a convincing alibi. Now, there is *no* way to get your *regular* doctor to treat you at home. If you lure him over with an alibi, he'll know he's been duped the second he arrives. He'll walk right out and you'll never see him again.

But there *is* a way to con a doctor who doesn't know you into making a house visit. Get the name of one from a friend or just pick one from the Yellow Pages who lives nearby. Dial his number and say: "Hello . . . Dr. So'n so? . . . I'm new in town, and the Chief of Internal Medicine* at Harvard back home recommended that I call you if I ever became sick. Would you please come right over?"

We'll give you odds that he'll be so flattered he'll come running!

Stingers for swingers

If you're the sort of man who finds monogamy monotonous, this has probably happened to you. A couple of hours after your wife has served dinnner, you arrive home reeking of your girl friend's perfume. Your olfactory responses have become so paralyzed that you're completely unaware of smelling like a lily. But your wife, who's been inhaling nothing stronger than the aroma of burnt meat loaf all night, is not so paralyzed. One sniff and she asks, "Since when have you taken to dabbing yourself with French perfume?"

Match fragrance with flagrance and reply boldly: "Isn't it awful? The Avon Lady dropped in at the office today and sprayed the joint!"

---

* Substitute any specialization that applies to what ails you, from Cardiology to Gynecology. If he asks the Chief's name, make one up. It's a thousand-to-one shot that he'll not recognize it.

Encore. What do you do if the same thing happens again?

You change your alibi: "Oh, honey, there was a demonstrator at Macy's spraying everyone who went by. I got spritzed."

Suppose she isn't satisfied and asks suspiciously, "And what were you doing at Macy's?"

No sweat. Just tell her: "One of the guys at my place wanted me to help him pick out a pipe to give his father-in-law."*

Switcheroo: If you've been cheating on your *mistress* and she smells perfume on you, all you have to do is shrug apologetically and say, "It's my wife's."

Brush up on your E.C.A.†

Your wife doesn't know it, but you and your secretary have been enjoying a torrid relationship. One evening you took her to dinner and, because she lives with her mother, parked on a dead-end street for a strenuous session of lovemaking.

The following day, your wife drives back from a shopping trip and says to you accusingly, "What's this doing

---

* Switch it to cigars if you aren't a pipe-smoker, or to any of your special interests: hi fi, sporting goods, and so on.

† Extra-Curricular Alibi-ability.

in the back seat of the car?" She holds up a pair of sexy panty hose!

Here's your wife-saver: "No wonder that garage was slow delivering my car yesterday. The attendant must have been having a ball in the back seat!"

The Ten Commandments for the extracurricular afficionado can be boiled down to a single commandment: "Thou shalt not get caught."

Never forget that what she doesn't know won't hurt her—or you. But if your conscience should bother you, remember the 11th Commandment: "Thou shalt ignore the other ten."

You were always a slob, but your wife notices that suddenly you've become very concerned about your appearance. You wear mod suits, jazzy ties, and splash yourself with cologne before going to work. One morning she eyes you suspiciously and asks, "Out with it, George—have you got a girlfriend?"

Do you ever! You're having a real wild time with the new bookkeeper. To put any such thoughts out of your wife's head, we suggest using the tête-à-tête tactic. Tell her, solemnly and confidentially: "Selma, I'm very embarrassed but I'm going to be perfectly truthful with you. I'm beginning to feel my age. My mirror tells me that Mother Nature is letting me down. But I'm not going to let *you* down, Selma. I fuss more over myself so that you'll be proud to have me around."

Prepare to brush away her tears of gratitude.

The telephone rings. Your wife answers, then hands it to you with a very cool, "She wants *Mr.* Sharp!"

The caller is a gal with whom you've been having an affair. "I know I shouldn't call you at home, darling," she purrs, "but I missed you *so* much. Can't you get out?"

You're in quite a spot, friend. You have to get the broad off the phone and come up with an alibi that will satisfy your wife (who's listening to every word and watching the expression on your face).

We have a real double-duty whammer for you. In a very annoyed voice, say: "No, I'm sorry, I can't possibly make it on such short notice."

Hang up abruptly and explain to your wife: "Imagine —they want to call an emergency business meeting to-night! I told them I'm not going."

Your wife will say, "Go, honey, go."

So now you can go!

When you come home from work, your wife confronts you with this alarming piece of news: "Nancy told me she saw you in the lingerie department at Bergdorf's today with a beautiful blonde—and she was trying on a sexy housecoat. Explain, please!"

This is no time to stammer and stutter. Without delay, de-fuse her distrust with this deception: "Well, now that the cat's out of the bag, I guess I'll have to own up. The girl Nancy saw works in my office. She's built exactly like you—height, weight, figure, just your size. She agreed to try on a housecoat I wanted to surprise you with. But I didn't like it on her and didn't think you'd like it, so I didn't buy it. Now that the surprise is out, want to go with me yourself and pick one out?"

You may have to part with a few bucks—but not with your wife.

You ask your wife to take your suit to the cleaners. Being a dutiful spouse, she first takes the trouble to see that your pockets are empty. Out of one pops a neat little package of contraceptives *and you don't use them* (at home, that is)! When she confronts you with her find, she doesn't have to say a word—but *you* do.

What's your excuse, playboy?

Easy does it: Here are three workable alibis we place at your disposal:

1) The don't-look-at-me gambit: "Oh, honey, I bought those for a young fellow in my office who was too shy to buy them himself. I'm bringing them in for him tomorrow."

2) The scapegoat technique: "Ha! Nice friends I have. They invite me to a bachelor party and then plant those things on me, that's their idea of a joke!"

3) The cunning convincer, especially effective on wives who covet their sex lives as much as their hus-

bands: "Aw gosh, darling, you spoiled my surprise. I thought it might be fun to act like kids again."

You're off the hook now, but next time empty your own pockets.

Your beautiful inamorata is becoming very possessive and impatient. She is in a rush for you to get divorced so you can marry her. But you know that her real interest in you is your money, and you have no intention of leaving your wife to marry her.

How do you put her off without losing a good thing?

Simply surmount the credibility gap by talking her language: "It wouldn't be fair to you if we got married now, baby, because I'd be penniless. You see, almost everything I own is in my wife's name. Give me time to transfer everything to *my* name."

That's called the give-the-gal-a-goal-to-shoot-for alibi!

You skipped lunch in favor of a matinee with the new steno at a nearby motel. When her emotions ran highest, she became overexcited—her fingernail marks are all over your back. You know that you're going to have to be ready with a P.F.A.* when you get home to your wife.

We have one that won't fail you. As soon as you return to the office, call your missus and say, "The boss

* Pre-Fabricated Alibi.

has asked me to duck out with him to the health club this afternoon. But I won't be home more than ten or fifteen minutes late."

That will set the stage for your grand coup. Later that night, when you slip into your pajamas and your wife detects your damaged dorsal epidermis, explain it by saying, "That's what I get for letting the rubber at the health club whack me with those twigs! It's barbaric!"

Your extracurricular date stood you up. Not knowing what else to do with the roses you'd brought along to put her in the mood, you take them home to your wife. Fool that you are, you forgot to remove the telltale card you stuck inside. Your surprised and delighted frau tears open the box, takes out the flowers, and then finds the damned card which reads: "For you, Jessica." The blood drains from her face as she snarls, "My name is Alice, or didn't you know!"

After you recover from the initial shock, do an about-face and start to laugh uproariously until she asks you what's so funny. Tell her: "Me and another guy at my place passed this florist. They had a special on roses and we decided to buy some for our wives. But it was so busy he waited on line while I wrote out the cards. I guess we got them mixed up. That's why I'm laughing. Imagine what his Jessica is going to say when she gets roses meant for my Alice!"

By expressing so much faith in Alice, she'll feel superior to Jessica, and she'll laugh, too.

When your wife's away, you like to play, especially with the well-stacked divorcée downstairs. Now that your wife is spending the night at her mother's house, you've sneaked this lonely and willing ex-Mrs. X up to your apartment.

But your dream of a big evening is shattered by the ringing of your doorbell. A glance through the peephole reveals your wife's canasta colleague from down the hall. She says, "I was waiting for the elevator when I heard Marge laughing. I figured she didn't go to her mother's after all so I thought I'd drop in."

If you're a chronic E.C.* games-player, you should have been prepared for such eventualities by purchasing an inexpensive cassette recorder and taping conversations with your wife "for sentimental reasons." Then all you have to do is keep the door shut and murmur sadly, "Gosh, no, Marge isn't here. What you heard was some tapes we made together. I'm such a sentimental slob I always play them when she's away."

Your unwelcome guest will leave, convinced you're the most devoted husband in town.

You didn't know it, but one of your wife's friends spotted you getting out of a cab with a fetching female at midday in midtown. But you find out when you arrive home and your wife puts you through the third degree.

Treat the incident with a cavalier attitude by saying

* Extra-Curricular.

with utter insouciance: "Oh, she got a job in my place and comes from out of town. She had to have a big check cashed in a hurry so I took her to my bank and vouched for her reliability with an officer I knew."

You did a good deed—just like a Boy Scout, *hmm*?

You're weekending with your wife at a resort hotel and are sauntering through the lobby by yourself when this gorgeous babe (with whom you've been moonlighting in the city) rushes over, throws her arms around you and plants a big kiss on your lips. Before you can even react, you spot your wife, her eyes agape. She's witnessed the incriminating incident!

Is there a way out short of hara-kiri?

Fortunately, yes. Give the babe a fast brush, then walk over to your wife and say, angrily: "That mean broad! I had to fire her last week and she swore she'd get me into trouble. I'm glad you *saw* what happened instead of *hearing* about it second hand and getting wrong ideas!"

That should strip away her suspicions.

Your mistress has you walking on air and you're so infatuated that you want to do the Santa Claus bit. So you taxi down to the most fashionable dress shop in town, have their models put on a private fashion show for you, then order three of their most expensive originals.

But as luck would have it, who is also on the scene but one of your wife's best friends! They're as close as Siamese twins, and you know that this intelligence will be relayed to your wife in less time than it takes to bounce a picture off Telstar.

How will you mollify your mystified missus when she demands an explanation? Don't sweat, because we have the puncture-proof alibi.

Just be gentle, germane, and genuine by telling her: "I had to stop in there, dear, to order some Paris originals as a favor to my old school chum Danny Drexler. He's now a struggling woman's wear manufacturer on the coast and wants to put out a line of low-cost dresses. Since he can't afford to hire a designer, he asked me to get him some high-fashion originals to copy—at his expense, of course. It may not be ethical but that's *his* problem."

P.S.: Your alibi may not be so ethical, either—but that's *her* problem.

Your wife opens your Diners Club statement and asks, "What's this bill from a florist? And this motel charge? I haven't gotten any flowers from you since we're married, and the only time you took me to a motel was to visit your cousin from Indiana!"

Don't fret, your marriage isn't *kaput*. The authors of this book, by virtue of their alibi training, are experts in marriage counseling. Our advice is to take that statement, scrutinize it under a bright light, then tell your wife: "This is remarkable, honey. Remember my mentioning Archie, the new guy in the office, to you? Well, he had a date with his girl and was flat broke so I let him borrow my credit card. He forged my name perfectly. Tomorrow I'll give him these bills and get the cash from him."

Our final advice is henceforth to have your credit card billings sent to your office address.

Your wife startles you one day by turning on that casual tone that spells trouble: "I have it on excellent authority that you lunched yesterday with a very attractive redhead. True or false?"

What's the point of denying it when you've been caught redhanded, not to mention redheaded?

Your only recourse is this route: "Absolutely true, dear. This restaurant used to be for men only. But Women's Lib got after them and they set up a new policy. Now every time a guy has a table by himself, he's forced to share it with any dame who comes in."

This demonstrates how a red-blooded male can use Women's Lib to his advantage.

Beware those tell-tale lipstick smears . . .

Your wife greets you at the door to bestow her usual welcoming kiss—but she stops short when she sees some other gal got there first! You forgot to check with your mirror before leaving your paramour after cocktails. Now your wife points to your face and demands: "All right, out with it . . . who kissed you?"

Our advice to you is—laugh it off and say: "It's nice to know you're jealous but you needn't be. The boss threw a small party for the steno. She's leaving to get married, and of course everybody kissed the bride-to-be."

In this case, you've just returned from a business trip. In between conferences, you managed to squeeze in a good time. But when your wife starts staring at your shirt, you realize you overlooked something, a very big something. In a hard and gritty voice, she asks: "What's that lipstick doing on your shirt?"

Relax. One of these alibis will get you off . . .

1) *If the smear is on the collar:* "Where? Oh . . . so that's why everyone's been staring at me today! That's *your* lipstick. You must've brushed your lips against this shirt while putting it away in my bureau."

2) *If the smear is on the top of the shirt:* "Oh, that's not lipstick. I was taking orders with the client's red marking pen and stuck it in the inside pocket of my jacket. It must have rubbed off."

Your wife has been emptying the hamper to gather up the dirty wash for the laundromat. Suddenly she calls out in a voice sodden with sarcasm: "Well, look what I found!" She walks over to you relaxing in your favorite easy chair and tosses on your lap one of your handkerchiefs—smeared with lipstick. And *she* knows it isn't *her* lipstick!

What whopper will you wangle your way out with?

Throw off her suspicions with this bit of hanky-panky: "One of the girls in the office got sick today and fainted. They brought her a glass of water and she started dribbling so I used my handkerchief to wipe her lips."

Your wife will be proud of your gallantry.

Wives swing, too . . .

In this case your boyfriend has given you a pair of golden earrings, studded with real diamonds. You tell your husband they're only costume jewelry ("brass and glass") that you picked up at the bargain center. But he discovers the truth when you wear them to a party and one of the guests, a jeweler, admires the earrings, pronouncing the gems and gold genuine. Your husband takes you aside and rages: "You lied and said they were fake! What have you been up to?"

You need a good story to get out of this jam, and here it is. As sheepishly as possible, say to him: "Yes, dear, I did lie. You see, mom and dad bought them for me and I knew you wouldn't want me to take such an expensive gift from them. I lied because I wanted the earrings but didn't want to hurt your feelings."

The poor guy will feel ashamed of himself for mistrusting you.

Another swinging story . . .

You're fortyish but your figure's still trim, and your boyfriend gifts you with some high-styled dresses to drape it with. You tell your husband that you got them in the bargain basement for next to nothing. Then one day he confronts you angrily: "All my friends laugh when I tell them you get your high-fashion clothes in the bargain basement! I want the truth!"

We suggest you "own up" and feed him this fooler: "I admit I didn't buy them, dear. *You* did—*years ago*! I've had them put away in mothballs and took them out now that the styles are back in fashion again."

If he asks why you didn't say that in the first place, just explain: "I didn't think you'd believe me."

Nifty swifties

The Nifty Swifty is an alibi that startles the hell out of people because it comes on so strong, so startling and so far out of left field.

You're eavesdropping on some juicy gossip in the powder room when suddenly one of the girls turns and says irately: "Getting an earful, busybody?"

Lean forward, cup your hand to your ear, and say loudly: "What?"

You faked a sprained foot to avoid running some rainy-day errands for your boss. At quitting time he spots you racing for the elevator and yells: "What happened to your limp?"

Reassure him: "Oh, the limp's still there. It just doesn't show because I took a codeine tablet and the pain let up."

Someone comes to your door for a contribution to some charity. You haven't a dime in the house.

Open the door a crack and say: "Sorry, the people are away. I'm only the painter."

You banged up the family car while shopping. When your husband sees the damage, he screams: "I thought you knew how to drive!"

Be petulant: "It's all your fault. You keep nagging me to fasten my seat belt. So when I took my hands off the wheel to do it, I missed a turn."

You're in the shoe store, about to try on a new pair of shoes. When the salesman slips one foot out of your old shoe, you're embarrassed to see a gaping hole in your sock.

Don't lose your cool. Merely exclaim: "How do you like that . . . my wife gave me my kid's socks again!"

You're an aging roué who's understated his age to impress a young widow. But while having a steak dinner at her apartment, your new dentures pop out. She's shocked and says accusingly: "You told me those were your own teeth!"

Pop 'em back in your mouth and reply: "They are, dear—and I have the paid in full receipt from my dentist to prove it."

You're a private secretary and are a half-hour late coming back to the office after lunch. Your boss demands to know why.

Tell him earnestly: "I couldn't help it. A man was following me and he walked very slowly."

You've just concluded a passionate liaison with your inamorata. She doesn't want you to go home to your wife, saying tearfully: "You're only interested in me for one thing."

Soothe her ego with this bit of flattery: "That's the one thing my wife wishes I was interested in *her* for!"

You're entertaining some visitors in your apartment. Suddenly one of the female guests drops her daquiri and screams: *"Eeeek!* A mouse!"

Act very unperturbed. With a wave of your hand, say: "Don't worry, that's not our mouse. He belongs next door and is only passing through."

You walk down the street with your wife and your head swivels every time a girl goes by. Very annoyed, your missus snaps: "Stop looking at other women!"

Accentuate the positive: "Why, dear? The more I look, the more I realize how lucky I am to be married to you."

You changed barbers. Now you bump into your old barber who says: "Where have you been? I haven't seen you in a long time."

Instead of being embarrassed, alibi: "Oh, I've been on the road a lot and have had to wait for planes. So I've been going to the airport barber shop to kill time."

How to blitz guest pests

Your alibi acumen is put to the test when you have to deal with an unwelcome guest. It's a knack that can be cultivated and no socially secure host or hostess can afford to be without it.

When unexpected guests ring your doorbell . . .

Identify them first by calling out, "Who's there?" If you don't feel like entertaining, yell, "Just a minute!" Then quickly wrap yourself in your bathrobe, throw a towel around your neck, and toss some water on your face to look like you're dripping sweat. Now that you're prepared, open the door and say, "Hi . . . better not come too close. I'm running a high fever."

They'll leave.

When guests overstay their welcome . . .

If it's *winter*, sneak down to the basement and turn up the heat as high as it will go. When the place begins to get uncomfortable, explain that the heating system is on the fritz and you're still waiting for the serviceman to show up. Grumble loudly about the discomfort and add that you can't even open the storm windows because they're sealed shut.

You'll sweat them out.

If it's *summer*, sneak down to the fusebox and unscrew the fuses that control the air conditioners and fans. The lights will go out, too, of course, adding to the confusion and discomfort. Pretend to investigate what happened by lighting matches to show the way to the basement. When you return, announce sadly: "It's not the house fuse. It must be trouble in the main circuits. We'll be stuck like this till morning."

They'll be glad to say good night.

If you live in a *big city*, hasten your guests' departure without offense by stealing a look at the time, then saying anxiously: "I'm getting worried. You know how dangerous the streets get late at night around here. Do you think you ought to go now while it's still safe?"

They'll be so nervous, they'll leave at once. See them off with this reminder: "Don't forget to give us a ring when you get home so we can breathe easier." That'll show them how concerned you are.

When your guests are waiting for an invitation to stay *overnight* . . .

If you can't bear to put up with them another day, you don't have to put them up for the night. All it takes is a bit of collusion between wife and husband. One goes out on the pretext of picking up a few goodies at the late-night deli. Let's say it's the wife. Once outside, she telephones home. The husband answers, pretends to be speaking to a friend, and appears very shocked. He hangs up and tells the guests, "That was my wife's best friend. Her husband just dropped dead. How am I going to break this news to my wife when she gets back? I know she'll just have to rush over there and comfort her."

The guests won't want to be involved in so personal a matter and will be gone before the wife gets back.

When you out-smart yourself . . .

You live in the suburbs. A friend is visiting you and

wants to make the 10:30 train back to the city. He becomes very edgy as the time approaches but you assure him that he'll make it. "There's no rush," you say. "This 10:30 train is always late. I know from experience that it has never, never been on schedule. Why, it's been known to be hours late."

Your friend stops worrying and you drive him to the station, arriving there at 10:35. Unfortunately, you discover that the 10:30 express left exactly on time. You have on your hands a frantic friend, cussing you out good.

Switch gears for a Tactical Maneuver. Act very surprised and tell your friend, "Wait here in the car for a moment." Then go into the station, pretending to talk to the stationmaster. Come out grinning smugly and say, "Just as I thought—that was yesterday's train!"

Now that you've saved face, prepare your wife for the prospect of having an overnight guest.

When *you* are the guest . . .

Some friends of yours bought an old farmhouse in New England and are reconverting it into a summer home. They invite you and your wife to come down for the weekend. It sounds like fun so you accept. But when you see the guestroom, you and your wife agree you want out. The room is still unfinished, it's hot, and the walls are made of fiberboard through which every sound can be heard throughout the house.

How can you squirm out of staying overnight and still spend both days with your hosts?

Take the husband aside and give him this "straight talk": "We appreciate your hospitality, Grover, but I have to tell you something just between us guys. I have this psychological thing where I just can't go to the bathroom in a strange house. So after dinner tonight, we'll stop at the motel down the road and come back in the morning to spend the day with you. Okay, pal?"

He'll respect your psychological hangup, and you'll spend a more comfortable night.

Trusty cop-outs to handle crusty cops

When you're stopped by a policeman for speeding, for passing a red light or for some other infraction, you'd better have an alibi ready and it had better be a good one. We're going to offer a few solid ones that you can use. Your choice will depend on such factors as the situation itself, the disposition of the cop, your ability as a convincing liar, who's in the car with you, and the number of bad marks on your driver's license.

1) You're doing 60, ten miles past the posted limit, across a busy bridge. Suddenly you hear the familiar

whine of a police siren. The next thing you know, a state trooper drives alongside you, commanding, "Pull over!"

You stop. He stops and comes swaggering over to your car. Very innocently, you say, "Why'd you make me pull over, officer?"

"For speeding 60 miles an hour, that's why!" he tells you.

Just point to the sign on the bridge—KEEP FIFTY FEET BEHIND NEAREST VEHICLE—and protest, "But I wasn't speeding, officer. I was only obeying the law and trying to catch up to the guy ahead of me."

This will also work in most tunnels.

2) Here's one for you lady drivers. Since traffic cops are generally anti-Women's Lib, you can be convincing if you act as expected: foolish and feminine.

You're on a deserted stretch of highway, anxious to get home and are really stepping on the gas. A cop comes zipping by on a motorcycle, motions to you to pull over, and of course you do.

"Lady," he says with some exasperation, "you were doing 70 miles an hour. What's the big hurry?"

Turn on all the feminine charm you possess, flick your artificial lashes, and say, "Truthfully, officer, my brakes aren't working too well and I wanted to get home before I had an accident."*

* This whopper was inspired by the late Gracie Allen who once alibied: "I'm low on gas and wanted to get home before I ran out."

policeman notices it when your car is parked in the shopping center lot and says threateningly, "It's illegal to have your license plate mounted upside-down!"

Can you avoid getting a summons?

You may if you placate the cop by murmuring: "Oh, I didn't mean to break the law, officer. I just did it for convenience' sake so I wouldn't have to roam all over the lot to find my car."

If he still insists on ticketing you, suggest to him that he write up this experience and send it to the Reader's Digest "Life in These United States" department. Remind him that they pay $100.00 for every acceptable contribution.

He'll put away his summons book.

When you're *not* driving . . .

It happens to everybody. You drive to the shopping center and find a parking spot with some time left in the meter. "Almost forty minutes left," you say to yourself. "If I can't get out of the store in forty minutes, I deserve a ticket!"

Well, when you finally emerge from the store—an hour later—you spot a Meter Maid starting to write down your license plate in her summons book. Your bravado's gone. After pinching pennies in the store, you don't want to get stuck with a fat fine.

This calls for fast action. Race over to that Meter Maid before she can get anything on paper. Then huff and puff as you pull out your wallet: "Look, Miss, I left my wallet in the store and had to go back for it because my driver's license is in it. And I wouldn't break the law and drive without a license."*

You're searching desperately for a parking spot so that you and your wife can make the last show at the movies. There isn't any space available except where parking is prohibited.

How can you park without chancing a ticket?

Believe it or not, there is a way. Simply let the air out of one tire—leaving it inflated just enough to get you to the nearest garage when the movie is over.† Then stick a note on your windshield: "Flat tire—have gone to garage."

No officer will ticket a car in trouble.

Celebrity alibis

To *W. C. Fields*, balderdash was a second language. He never made the mistake of resorting to the truth when an alibi would serve his purpose. His alibis were wildly ridiculous but, served up in the elegant style that made him famous, got him off the hook.

* If you wear eyeglasses, you can use this switcheroo. Pull out your specs and say: "I left them on the counter, Miss, and I had to go back fast to get them because I can't drive without glasses."
† If you carry one of those spray can tire inflators in your trunk, you can let out all the air.

When a fellow performer asked him for a loan, Fields replied: "Ordinarily, I would be only too happy to oblige you. Unfortunately, I am now in the strange situation of having all my available funds completely tied up in ready cash."

A great ping pong addict, Fields wagered heavily on every game. One time, when playing Humphrey Bogart, he deliberately shook the table, forcing Bogey to net his shot, and then exclaimed: "It was an earthquake! One of the hazards of California living. This table is squarely over the San Andreas fault."

Comedian *Jackie Mason* claims that he was out driving one afternoon when a traffic policeman drove up beside him and yelled, "Hey, do you know you're doing 60 miles an hour?"

With a shake of his head, Jackie replied: "That's ridiculous, officer. I'm not even on the road an hour."

Joe E. Lewis, the great nightclub comic, gave a chum a hot tip on a horse. After the race, the guy came over to Joe E. fuming, "You told me that was a great horse. He came in last!"

Joe E. looked surprised and said: "That proves he was a great horse. It took eleven other horses to beat him."

TV star *Garry Moore* receives an occasional crank letter from a disgruntled fan. He has a standard response, answering all such mail this way: "Dear Sir: The enclosed letter arrived on my desk a few days ago. As a responsible citizen, I thought you ought to know that some idiot is sending out mail over your signature."

When the late *George M. Cohan* phoned to make a hotel reservation, he was asked how he spelled his last name. Afterward, he realized the hotel was restricted. He then sent this wire to the management: "You thought I was Jewish, and I thought you were American. We were both wrong. Cancel reservations."

Movie actor *David Niven* was lunching out with some friends when a curvy young female came rushing over, gushing, "David!" He hadn't the slightest idea who she was but didn't want to embarrass her or himself.

Thinking fast, he jumped up, kissed her hand and cried, "Darling!" Then he turned to his companions, saying, "She's all mine, and I shan't share her with any of you." He led the glowing gal away, chatted briefly with her, then kissed her hand again and bid her goodbye. She departed on a cloud.

When his friends asked why he'd swept the girl away as if they wanted to abduct her, he explained: "You'll have to forgive me. I couldn't remember who the devil she was and I couldn't take a chance."

When a male admirer comes up to sultry *Mae West*, asking, "Remember me?" and Mae doesn't, she stares into the guy's eyes and says seductively, "Well, I may have forgotten your name but I'll always remember your eyes."

If you don't catch the new flesh films making the scene, you aren't apt to be considered gung-ho with the "in" crowd. But you can preserve that sophisticated veneer the crowd prizes so highly with a few choice alibis to explain why you haven't seen the pictures.

Goodman Ace, who shares your taste, uses these with great success:

"I don't like to stand and wait in long lines."

"The show is over so late, I'm out on a dark, deserted street, walking home, and who knows what can happen?"

"I miss the breaks for the commercials we get on TV."*

If you know nothing about football, and your date has tickets to the game, it's important not to show your ignorance. Take a tip from football immortal *Benny Friedman* and do this: "When you see a player running with the ball, and the crowds cheering, don't say anything. Your beau will think you an expert if you say only: *'Boy, did you see that tackle take out that guard!'* "

You'll make his Hall of Fame with that kind of know-how.

---

* Goody likes this one especially and sometimes adds: "Sitting for two hours in a movie without some messages thrown at you can be hazardous to your health."

If you're the kind who likes to lop years off your age to appear younger, don't make the mistake actress *Joan Blondell* did. When she was married to *Dick Powell*, he advised her to subtract five years from her age for publicity purposes.

She subtracted five from the *year of her birth*, 1914! That's why the motion picture "Who's Who" lists her birthday as 1909.

Now she really needs an alibi.

The invisible millionaire, *Howard Hughes*, concocted a clever (and expensive) alibi to break a date. The *modus operandi* was a long distance call *from* Los Angeles *to* Los Angeles. Here's how he did it:

He and the girl were *both* in L.A. He made a long distance call to the Madison Hotel in New York. When he got the switchboard operator, he asked her to hold *him* on the wire, then to put through a *long distance call* to the girl in L.A. and *cut him in* so he could talk to her—presumably from the Madison Hotel in New York.

When she did that, Hughes told the girl he couldn't keep the date because *he* was in New York. She said, "I don't believe you. I just saw you yesterday." Hughes replied, "Okay! I'll prove it. Hang up and call me back at the Madison Hotel to convince yourself, and charge the call to me." She did so and the hotel operator put her through to him on the line she was holding open from L.A. Hughes polished off his brilliant ploy by telling the contrite young woman, "Now I hope this will be the last time you'll mistrust me."

When *George Horace Lorimer* edited the old *Saturday Evening Post*, the magazine began to run serials that shocked some of its readers. The first installment sometimes ended with the heroine having a drink with a married man. The second installment would then begin with the two having breakfast together.

Lorimer answered indignant readers with a form letter that demonstrated alibiing at its very best: "The *Post* cannot be responsible for what the characters in its serials do between installments."

H. L. Mencken, the celebrated American wit, was so swamped with controversial letters that he had no time even to read them. He devised an alibi that made reading them unnecessary.

To every letter writer, he replied courteously: "Dear Sir (or Madam): You may be right."

On the *Tonight* show, *Johnny Carson* hosted *Baby Rose Marie* (as she was known years ago when she was a child singing star). In trying to indicate diplomatically that many years had elapsed since her debut, he groped for the right words and kept getting himself in deeper and deeper. Rose Marie sat silently smiling. Suddenly, she got up and walked offstage, and the other guests followed her off, leaving Carson with egg on his face while the audience howled.

Carson looked around at the bare stage, chuckled, and alibied: "I thought they'd never leave."

How to skin friends and insolent people

As the great poet Longfellow once wrote in his scrapbook: "When someone wants to borrow something you don't want to lend, you'd better have an alibi or you won't have a friend."

The only other alternative is to lend whatever it is in spite of yourself. This is what started all the trouble back in the Garden of Eden. When Adam asked Eve for a bite of her apple, she handed it over to avoid hurting his feelings. We'd have all been better off if she had alibied: "Okay, Adam, but there's a worm in it."

Sometimes you have to embarrass yourself to discourage a moocher. You believe in the good neighbor policy, but the neighbor down the street has abused her privilege. If you didn't keep track of what you lent her, you'd never get anything back. Now she wants to borrow some of your good chairs for a party.

How do you send her scurrying elsewhere?

Swallow your pride and say politely: "You can have them, dear, but I must warn you—we've been invaded by silverfish and they got into everything!"

Now *she'll* have to think of a polite alibi to refuse the chairs.

This is for our Jewish readers . . .

An acquaintance approaches you one Saturday morning and asks you to lend him twenty bucks. You don't want to turn him down flat.

What we suggest you do is put him off this way: "On Saturday? I don't handle money on the Sabbath. Ask me tomorrow."

The next day he'll call and ask. But you're prepared. All you have to say is: "Why didn't you call earlier? I just gave my last twenty bucks to my brother-in-law."

This is for anybody . . .

An old friend asks you for a substantial loan. If you turn him down, he'll never forgive you. If you give him the dough, it's Goodbye Charlie.

How can you get off the hook?

Tell him, in a businesslike way: "I'll have to talk it over with my tax man."

Nine out of ten times he'll get the message. But if he does follow through, just tell him: "I had my accountant check out my financial position and he says if I make any major withdrawals now, I'll louse up my whole tax situation."

A friend wants to borrow your brand-new car for a couple of hours. That's a couple of hours too long as far as you're concerned.

How can you turn him down?

What you need is a rejoinder that has the ring of truth. Here it is: "I'd like to lend you the car, Bruce, but my insurance company won't let me. My policy has a restrictive clause and only my wife and I are covered as drivers. If you drive it, I'll be liable for all damages and will lose the policy."

He'll take off on foot.

The only thing harder to find than a doctor who'll make housecalls is a maid. Naturally, if you're fortunate to engage one for a couple of days a week, all your friends will want to "borrow" her on the days she doesn't work for you. This could be a dangerous good deed. If you lend her to a woman who has a smaller house to do, is less demanding or will pay her more than you do, you'll lose her services for good.

But how do you turn down a friend without telling her you're worried that she'll steal your girl away from you?

Here are some alibis guaranteed to keep your greed intact:

"She's great with kids but terrible at housework."

"She's not bad at housework but hates children."

"She won't scrub or mop but she's good company."

"Whenever she works, we have to empty the freezer or she's empty it into her stomach."

"She's always on the telephone, so if you don't have two phones, forget it."

You know your customers. Choose your weapon—knock the qualities most wanted and the ladies will be loath to let you lend her.

Friendship and femininity . . .

When a woman's notion of what's feminine is at stake, she has to lie. Sometimes she uses visual lies. If she's built like a stickball bat, she'll wear falsies. If she's homely, she'll have her teeth capped, wear a wig that gives her more flair, and substitute contact lenses for spectacles. If her age is showing, she'll buy a more youthful wardrobe, smear her face with make-up to conceal the wrinkles or have plastic surgery done if she can afford the expense.

If someone accuses her of putting on weight, she'll alibi, "My husband likes me with more meat on my bones. He says it makes me sexier."

If she can't afford to dress stylishly, she'll alibi, "I like to be an individualist and dress the way I want, not the way some fashion-designer tells me to."

If she has to shop for sales to save pennies, she'll alibi, "It's a matter of principle."

If her husband never takes her anywhere, she'll alibi, "We love to stay home together."

If her kids are rotten little monsters who bully other children, she'll alibi, "My psychiatrist told me not to stifle them."

And if she has to work to make ends meet, she'll alibi, "I believe it's heathier to have outside interests."

How can you keep a nose job secret?

Tell everyone you're starting on a skiing holiday the day you're scheduled for surgery. Be sure that you're seen leaving with your bag and skis. Then drive off—to the hospital.

After your nose bob, there'll be some bandages taped across your schnozz. Have the nurse wrap a few more around a leg, a hand, and improvise a little sling for your arm. When you arrive home from the hospital, tell everyone: "I'm through with skiing forever. I got all banged up and broke my nose in the bargain, and they had to reset it."

Remove the phony bandages *before* you finally exhibit your new nose. By then everybody will have bought your alibi and their only reaction will be: "Gee, the doctors did a marvelous job. You look great!"

How can you keep a middle-age facelift secret?

Spread the word that you're off to the Riviera or some other holiday haven, but take a detour to your plastic surgeon.

When you return home with your refurbished face, demolish the skeptics with: "What a place, what a climate, what a vacation! It lopped years off my age—I only hope it shows!"

It does, it does.

To impress the girls attending your ladies club luncheon, you serve them a special cheesecake which your husband brought home from a gourmet shop in the city. You boast that you made it yourself. But the cheesecake scores such a big hit all the femmes are clamoring for the recipe!

If you won't give it to them, you'll be exposed as a

culinary fraud. And you can't even wing it, because you haven't the foggiest as to the ingredients!

Employ a ruse that makes it impossible for you to accommodate them. We call this the Alas-and-Alack Alibi.

In a regretful voice, say: "I'm ashamed to admit it, but this is the first time that cake came out right. I changed the entire recipe as I went along—but I stupidly forgot to write down what I did differently!"

How can you give them the recipe for an 'ad lib' cake?

Your lost cake will go down in history like the Lost Chord.

Your new dress makes such a hit that you can't resist telling everyone you made it yourself. Actually, you had it made by an expensive dressmaker. But one of your neighbors is so impressed by "your" work that she wants you to join her weekly sewing circle and teach the girls a few tricks.

You're trapped. You can't even thread a needle. Must you admit you lied?

Certainly not. The thing to do is lie again! Put on an unhappy look and reply: "I have to tell you something. It was all I could do to finish this dress. My arthritis has been so bad that my sewing days are over."

When friends are demanding . . .

Your friend's hippie son wants to use you as a reference for a job. This doesn't set too well with you because this bearded, bushy-haired kid in beads and ragged jeans is not only unreliable, he's also incapable.

How do you refuse him without offending him?

You can weasel out with an ambiguous answer if he tells you his prospective employer will get in touch with you. Just shrug: "I'll be glad to tell him what I think of you."

On the other hand, you may prefer to discourage any phone calls or letters. To accomplish this, you have to get the point across that even your best reference will do more harm than good.

Can you guess how?

Simple. When he tells you the name of his prospective employer, grimace and say: "I'll be glad to give you a reference, Abbie, but I have to warn you ... the guy who owns that company hates my guts! If you mention my name, it'll be the kiss of death."

If that doesn't turn him off, nothing will.

When friends are envious ...

There's been a garbage strike in your community for over a week. Garbage is piled up in front of everyone's house—except yours. Naturally, they're all wondering what you do with yours. Well, you're a real shrewdie. You've been giftwrapping your garbage in beribboned boxes, placing them on the front seat of your car in the driveway, and leaving the car windows open. Each morning the packages are gone—obviously stolen by thieves who think they've made off with a bonanza!

You've got too good a thing going to give it away to your neighbors. So, when they ask what you do with your garbage, squirm out with this subterfuge: "Oh, I just take it over to the dump early every morning."

They'll be down in the dumps until the strike is over.

Those "friendly" digs . . .

You made a big thing about giving up smoking but after three weeks of self-deprivation you're back on the butts again. You know, sooner or later, some "pal" is going to see you light up and say something deprecating like: "Poor old Charlie, no will power, eh?"

Be prepared with a good alibi and you needn't feel embarrassed. Here's one we know will work because we've used it. Simply tell the guy: "It's not too little *will* power, but too much *diet* power that's got me back on cigarettes. I joined a diet club and they told me I'd better start smoking again or I'll never be able to stick to my diet."

Everybody knows that when you quit smoking, you eat more. It works the other way around, too.

Your husband phones to say he'll be working late and not to expect him for dinner. So you make a date with a girlfriend to join you in dinner out. By one of those weird coincidences that always happens at the wrong time, you choose the same restaurant where your husband is dining—with a beauteous blonde! Your friend also sees him and her eyebrows go way up.

How do you explain the blonde to your friend to keep her from making gossip?

Take charge of the situation firmly and whisper: "Oh my goodness, there's Jack with the vice-president of his firm. She's a notorious lesbian, you know. But he has to put up with these after-hours dinner conferences to keep his job. Let's go someplace else so we won't embarrass him."

Lead her away quickly before Jack spots *you*.

It was inevitable. Your husband hired a stunner as his Gal Friday. You're simmering, of course, but don't dare let your friends in on your true feelings. So what's your answer when someone gives you the needles and asks if you're jealous?

Without a moment's hesitation, come right back with: "Jealous? Are you kidding? I'm delighted. Now Sheldon won't *dare* come home late for dinner any more!"

That'll blunt their needles.

This manual for mendication wouldn't be complete if we didn't offer a workable whopper to answer that hardy old perennial: "Who gave you that black eye?"

Okay, so it was your wife (or husband), but naturally you want to shun that kind of admission. Here are several effective shiner shunners that deal with the incident more imaginatively. Take your pick . . .

1) "That's what comes of squeezing my eye against a telescope half the night. I've taken up astronomy, you know."

2) "My wife and I got lost driving home from the country late Saturday night. I made her take the wheel while I read a roadmap with the help of a flashlight. Suddenly she stopped short and the damn flashlight hit me square in the eye!"

3) "Nobody gave me this shiner. My liver has been acting up."

4) "I was having my eyes checked at the ophthalmologist's. He swung a big instrument around for me to look into and it slipped out of his hand—right into my eye. And on top of everything, he charged me for the visit!"

Speaking of freak accidents, one of the authors of this book did K.P. duty in the Air Force and drew the job of grinding up cooked fish for fishcakes. The meat-grinder handle came loose and socked him in the eye. But he didn't have to cop out because everyone thought he had a case of "bombardier's eye": a black eye that comes from peering through the bombsight when the plane hits an airpocket, causing a severe jolt to the eye by the bombsight.

Win when you lose

To reach the exalted rank of Compulsive Alibi Freak, you have to know how to turn the tables on other people. Stun them with the unexpected. Make them feel ridiculous. Arouse feelings of self-doubt, shame or guilt. Here are some quick and easy lessons to show how it's done.

You take out the new car and dent the fender. Your husband is fit to be tied.

Solicit his sympathy with this master-stroke of mendication: "Aren't you glad that speeder only *clipped* me and I'm back home safe and sound!"

He'll feel like a worm for complaining.

The dame is drippy but you date her only when you're desperate. Now she complains that she's heard you've been downgrading her to other guys and saying she's not passionate.

Fan her femininity with this flattering fib: "Can you blame me for discouraging the competition so I can have you all to myself?"

She'll be plenty passionate that P.M.

You're undergoing the ordeal of a tax audit. You begin to sweat as the examiner gets into the sensitive area of charitable deductions and scrutinizes each item. If you don't distract him, you're in trouble.

Cross your fingers and pant: "Please, I'd appreciate it if you'd hurry up. My tranquillizer is beginning to wear off."

Chances are he'll chuckle and stop trying to nail you.

You've been pushing a special diet bread on your friends because your husband has an interest in the company. One day an especially plump gal stops you and says, "That bread's not helping me. I haven't lost a pound."

Cast doubts upon her conclusion by commenting: "That's because you don't eat enough of it."

That will seem reasonable to a dieter in search of magic.

One of those super-patriots brags to you, "My ancestors came over on the Mayflower. Did yours?"

Stop him with this squelcher: "No, they missed the boat. And by the time they decided to come over, the immigration laws were tighter."

He may snicker but that'll bother him all night.

You've been lopping years off your age. One day an acquaintance stops you cold by saying sarcastically, "I hear you have a daughter in college. And you're only 30?"

Meet impudence with impudence: "If you must know, we adopted her when she was twelve!"

She'll want to crawl into a hole in the ground.

Your wife serves you cookies for dessert. You assume she got them at a bakery and comment, "These are pretty bad." She retorts icily, "I baked them myself!"

Bounce right back with this beguiler: "You didn't let me finish, dear. These are pretty bad *for my diet*."

Ten to one she asks your forgiveness for jumping the gun.

A demonstrator tries to pin a button on you. Flag or Peace symbol, you don't want it.

Divert him with this disclaimer: "Thanks, old chap, but I'm only visiting here from abroad."

Even if your accent's weak, he'll give you the benefit of the doubt.

You're nightclubbing with your wife and along comes the club's girl photographer. She offers to snap a Polaroid picture of you and the missus for a mere five bucks. Turn her down, and you'll look like a tightwad. How do you handle this shakedown?

Wink at her slyly and whisper: "Not tonight—she's not my wife."

The photog will get the picture—but not the snapshot.

You know a guy who's trying to give up smoking by mooching other people's cigarettes. Well, with the price of butts so high it's gotten to be a pretty expensive mooch.

The next time he tries to grub a smoke, here's the way to shaft him: take out a pack that has only one cigarette in it and say, "Gee, I'm down to my last one and was just about to light up."

Of course, your *regular* full pack is in another pocket—but the grubber doesn't know that. He'll search for another sucker.

A lulu lie can save your job

The lie you fail to tell today may mean the job you fail to keep tomorrow. Alibiing should come as naturally to the wage slave as it does to the boss. We offer here some exercises in exemplary excuses.

Your boss would like your son to date his homely daughter but the kid won't do it, even for you. How do you explain this to your boss?

Tell him with unabashed sincerity: "That boy of mine is a nice kid but at a stage where he tries to prove his manhood with every girl he meets. So I've forbidden him to ask your lovely daughter out until he's sown his wild oats."

The boss won't want him to sow any wild oats in *his* garden.

You get some hot tips on the horses and decide to take the day off to go to the track. So you call in sick, then off you go. When you reach your seat in the grandstand, you discover that someone else had the same idea: your boss! He looks you up and down, growling, "You sure made a quick recovery!"

This calls for a Quick Recovery Alibi, and it has to be good. This one is: "I'm sorry, boss, but I had to come here. You see, my wife's a nut on astrology. Last night she read my chart and said this would be the luckiest day of my life. She insisted I go to the track and just play my hunches."

Any fellow gambler—even one's boss—will comprehend that logic.

One of your jobs as a private secretary is to keep pesky salesmen out of your boss' office. For this challenging task, you need an arsenal of alibis. Here are some you can use . . .

1) "You just missed him. He's been in but went out again."

2) "He's somewhere in the building but I don't know where, and I don't know when he'll be back."

3) "He's in an awful grouchy mood today. I'd stay out of his way if I were you."

4) "You must have passed him in the hall. He took off early today."

You've been carrying on a daily gin rummy game with the buddy who shares your office. Every afternoon, at 4:30, out comes the deck of cards, score pad, and pencil, and the play resumes.

But alas, one day the Boss barges in and catches you both red-handed, just as you are about to knock with five points!

How do you avoid being blitzed by the boss for your goldbricking?

Now hear this: Simply tell him—"J.J., you won't believe this, but Al and I were delegated by the rest of the office to shop for your Xmas present. (Or birthday present, if you know the date and it's close.) We disagreed what to get you, so we decided to play a game of gin—and the winner gets the privilege of buying you what he thinks you'd like best."

Such puffery is bound to win a sympathetic reaction. If he wants to kibitz, let him.

The office grapevine has it that the boss has taken off for the day, so you decide to cut out an hour before quitting time. Precisely at four, you're out in the hall in your hat and coat, awaiting the elevator. When the door opens, you do a double-take—out comes your boss, apparently returning from a meeting! One look tells you things went badly and are kicking up his ulcer. Without so much as a hello, he roars, "Who gave you the day off?"

Should you hand in your resignation then and there?

Not with alibi artists like us working for you. Just do another double-take and exclaim, "My gosh, that joker wasn't fooling . . . his trick really worked!" That'll stop your employer dead. Now go right into an explanation: "I was at a party last night and one of the guests was an amateur hypnotist. For laughs, I let him hypnotize me. The last thing I recall him saying was—'Tomorrow at exactly four o'clock you will get up from your desk, put on your hat and coat, and go home early.' It's spooky!"

We can't guarantee this will work more than once.

You come back to the office from an unsuccessful business trip. Now you're on the carpet for failing to land the account.

What's your alibi?

Here are several nuggets that we've mined for you. Choose the one that comes most naturally: "Boss, I didn't land the account because . . ."

"Nader's Raiders were casing the joint and the place was a madhouse."

"The Shriners were in town and everyone was looped."

"The Internal Revenue auditors were going over their books and the boss was on the verge of apoplexy."

"Nobody was in the mood to do business. The V.P.'s wife caught him cheating and was in the office raising a ruckus."

Tele-phonies

A *Tele-Phony* is an alibi made possible by AT&T. It has a built-in advantage in that there is no personal confrontation. The other party is separated from you by miles of wire and bad connections.

The phone rings. You pick it up. The minute your party says hello, you recognize him as the pest who's been trying for days to pin you down to lunch or cocktails.

How do you shake him?

Give him the Lightning Lie treatment. The idea is to hit him so fast you take his breath away. Clip him off midsentence: "Oh, Don, I was just reaching for the phone to call the airport when you rang. Have to catch the first plane to London. Big deal, you know. So would you please hang up so I can make my call? Thanks, old buddy."

Hang up and smile.

That same guy calls you up for a date. You've already broken several dates with him so you'd better have a good excuse to turn him down now.

The phone is your salvation. In a very weak voice, tell him, "Joel, I know I said I'd be free for lunch today. But please, can we skip it? All of us at the office just came back from the blood bank, it was our turn to give. And I have to rest for a while, so I'm eating in."

You wouldn't get away with this if he could see the color in your cheeks. You were saved by the Bell System.

Your wife answers the telephone. On the line is a prominent local politico who's a nonstop talker. You cannot stand the guy but he's a valuable business contact and so you have to put up with him. When your wife calls you to the phone, she hollers, "Telephone, dear! It's the old windbag again!" But she forgets to cover the mouthpiece. He heard every word.

Do you have to write him off as an ex-contact?

Not at all. It's a perfect spot to pull the old mistaken identity trick—but with a difference. As soon as you get on the phone, say, "Hello, Pete." Wait for a response, then exclaim, "Oh, it's *you*, Dave! My wife thought you were my cousin Pete. He always bends my ear."

That should bring you—and your wife—back into his good graces.

Want to get rid of a bore who won't get off the phone? It's easier than you think. As soon as you can get a word in, start talking—then hang up on yourself in the middle of a sentence!

No egomaniac will suspect that anyone would hang up on himself. The conceited caller will simply assume that he's been victimized by a typical telephone company snafu. Hammer home this delusion by taking the phone off the hook so that if the caller tries to phone back, he'll get a busy signal.

Want to get a day off from work to enjoy yourself?

It's child's play with the help of an accomplice and the telephone. Arrange with your wife (or someone else) to call you at your job. When she does, just say, "Yes . . . okay . . . right . . . I'll be there."

Then hang up and tell your curious co-workers, "How do you like that! The Internal Revenue people want me down there Friday to go over my tax return."

The crocodile tears will flow like wine—and you can bet that your boss will join in, because misery loves company. And you can enjoy a long weekend.

Want to know how to get rid of an obscene phone-caller? Here are two tested techniques:

1) The Mechanical Gambit

When you hear that dirty rasping voice, don't panic. Just press down the telephone-cradle button quickly, two times, and then say matter-of-factly: "Officer, this is the call I want traced."

You won't be disconnected, but the caller will think a cop is listening in on the line. He'll hang up fast.

2) The Change-of-Voice Gambit

This was used effectively by comedienne Lily Tomlin who plays the role of Ernestine the Telephone Operator on the Rowan and Martin TV Show "Laugh-In." When she received an obscene phone call at her New York hotel room, she switched to her Ernestine voice and said, "Sorry, sir, but your call has been interrupted by trouble on the line. Please hold on and you'll be re-connected."*

While the caller waited, she ran next door to her manager's room, told her to phone the cops and trace the call, then went back to the phone. She kept him on the line long enough for the police to trace him to a phone-booth in Brooklyn and arrest him.

Here are three tested throttlers guaranteed to make the caller cut the conversation short:

1) "I'd like to go on gabbing but I have someone on the other phone."

2) "As much as I hate to, I have to get off. I'm expecting a long distance call."

3) (*If it's early*) "We're still sleeping."†

When Joe Franklin, the TV talk show host, doesn't want to talk to someone, he uses either of these two alibis:

---

* You can stop right here because he might get scared and hang up. If not, you can hang up. He won't have the nerve to call back.
† This should cover you till 2:00 P.M.

1) Hands the phone to an associate, saying, "Tell him I have a sore throat and can't talk."

2) Takes the call himself, and says, "Hello? . . . Uh . . . I'm just rushing out to tape my show. I'll call you Saturday between two and six."

Of course, Saturday never comes.

Publishers call him frequently to book their authors on his program. He never says no even when he means no. Polite Joe uses this alibi: "How long will he be in town? . . . Uh-huh . . . Okay . . . Contact me next time he's in New York because I'm doing reruns for the rest of the week. Keep in touch."

Your wife gives you a message that a Mr. Cohn called and wants you to call him back. But he's someone you prefer to avoid so you decide not to return his call. A few days later, however, he catches you in and asks, "I left a message with your wife that Mr. Cohn called. Didn't she give it to you?"

Slip him the stunner: "Cohn? The name she gave me was *Stone!*"

Switcheroo: You can also use the *first* name to cop out: *"Sam* Cohn? And I've been trying to reach *Joe* Cohn for days! Next time leave your first name."

Did you ever try to reach the top executive of a large company and have his private secretary refuse to put him on because he doesn't know you?

Next time, cut her short with this shocker: "Never mind who I am. You just tell him I want to find out what he's doing with my wife!"

He'll pick up the phone pronto. He'll start off spittin' mad, but after you explain the reason for your ruse, he'll chuckle and admire your ingenuity.

Did you ever want to get back at the telephone company because of lousy service?

Create your opportunity by not paying your bill for three months. The company will then threaten to take action. *Don't call them. Write*: "Please be patient with us. We are temporarily unable to send you a check. Our bookkeeper is out of order. We tried calling you about our difficulty. We know you will understand."

If they try to telephone *you* about that letter, just say: "Sorry, you have a wrong number." And when the phone rings again, don't answer.

Party smarties

You're hosting a festive Thanksgiving dinner for eight VIP's. When the maid comes in proudly bearing the turkey on a silver tray, she trips, and the tray falls to the floor.

Do you serve your guests potluck?

Not on your life. Just tell the maid: "Dora, pick up the turkey and please bring in the other one!"

And give thanks to the publisher who made this book possible.*

It's a real swinging party and your buddy's wife is beginning to look pretty tempting. Riding high on Rob Roys, you make a pass. What you overlooked is the hard fact that your buddy is a very jealous character.

So what do you do when he zooms in out of nowhere and catches you holding her hand?

Bail yourself out with this bamboozler: "Hey, Fred, did I tell you I've taken up palmistry? Watch me tell her fortune."

Also tell her that her lifeline shows her marriage will be happy.

You've had one of those point-of-no-return spats with your wife, and you're both due to show at a friend's dinner party in two hours. But the iceberg atmosphere can't be defrosted, and all the tea in China won't make you bury the hatchet with your wife. Still, you have to get off the hook about disappointing your friend.

We have three goodies to save your bacon. Just dial your friend's number and choose whichever suits you best:

* And to novelist Fannie Hurst who proved the alibi works.

1) "Hey, George, guess what? We were just about to leave and drive to your house when suddenly we noticed that our car had been stolen. Someone must have released the brakes and rolled it away. Now we're waiting for the cops."*

2) "Listen, I'm in terrible shape. I just stepped out of the shower, took a shave, and suddenly noticed I misplaced my dentures. With three front teeth missing, I look like the wreck of the Hesperus. I know you'll understand."†

3) "Oh gosh, you'll never guess what happened. The wife and I planted some stuff in the garden the other day and we've both come down with poison ivy. Right now we look like Indians covered with warpaint. And oh the itching!"‡

You give a smashing party for a dozen friends and the next day bump into the one gal you didn't invite. She lowers the boom on you in sneaky fashion, saying, "I saw a lot of cars in front of your house last night." That lets *you* know that *she* knows.

Don't pop your cork. Just pop her with this pip: "Oh, those were some people I've been promising to see for months. It wasn't your kind of party and I wouldn't

---

* Phone him back a few days later to inform him that the police found your car abandoned by some joy-riders.

† Be sure to *lisp* when you tell this one.

‡ A contagious disease beats a headache ten to one when you want to cop out.

dream of putting you through it. Everybody brought their own of everything, from booze to baloney. My next party's going to be a dandy and I want you to come and just bring yourself."

That should keep you in her good graces.

Extra: If you should happen to omit her from your guest list in the future, dismiss the oversight with: "It wasn't really a party, just a reunion of my old college chums. Even my husband felt left out of things."

You're visiting some friends out of town and they take you along to a party. They're a very cultured bunch, especially about music. In an effort to impress the crowd, you drop a few hints about your ability as a guitarist. The truth of the matter is that you plunk away like a rank amateur. But to your dismay, the host suddenly whips out a guitar and invites you to play something.

How are you going to extricate yourself from this embarrassment?

Be nonchalant, be firm, but also be apologetic: "Sorry, I'd like to entertain you but I make it a rule never to play impromptu without rehearsing beforehand. My reputation, you understand."

Would Segovia do otherwise?

You invited some pals to your pad for a party. One uninhibited character makes right for your liquor cabinet to search out the Scotch. All he can find is a cheap label and blurts out: "Hey, what's this? Where's the good stuff?"

Now, you really did cheap out, an unwilling victim of financial necessity, but you can't tell anybody that. Instead, use our Save-the-Day Sizzler: "This *is* the good stuff. But to keep my free-loading pals from drinking it up on me, I pour it into other bottles. Smart, eh?"

Take our word for this—he'll believe you even after he tastes the booze. Most people really can't tell one brand from another.

The party's going on full tilt but you're oblivious to everything. You've made it to the terrace with someone else's luscious wife. Her chin is cupped between your two trembling hands as you're about to plant a large wet kiss on those beckoning lips. Suddenly those lips begin to move and form the alarming words: "My husband is right behind you."

This could be messy if you didn't have this book to bail you out. Here's the antidote: stay as you are, don't turn your head, and just say out loud, "Nope, I can't find a thing in your eye. Better go see a doctor."

The stalking husband will stop stalking. He'll be grateful—and so will his wife.

You threw a big bash one evening but had no idea that one of your guests was a deadbeat. You find out when your phone bill arrives with a whopping $28.00

charged for long distance calls the night of the party. You know that you never called the places listed and it doesn't take long for you to figure out who was responsible. Only one gal in the crowd has relatives in those cities.

How can you make her pay the bill without creating hard feelings?

Put her in her place politely. Send her the bill, circling the charges, and pen a "friendly" note that says: "Dear Angela ... I'm afraid the phone company didn't follow your instructions. They stupidly charged these calls to our phone instead of yours."

Sign it: "Love."

This jawboning will work, even though she knows you're lying through your teeth.

How to avoid time-wasters

You can always duck out of a dull affair or business meeting by setting up a good alibi in advance. As soon as you walk in, announce to everyone: "I can't stay long because ..."*

"I have to pay a fine in traffic court before noon."

"My insurance company notified me that there's a lien

* Choose the one that's most appropriate.

against my house and I have to run down to the county courthouse and examine the records."

"Last night I noticed that my car's inspection sticker had expired and I have to rush to an official station to get it inspected."

"They just called me from the railroad station to tell me that someone turned in my attaché case. I have to be at their Lost and Found department before five to claim it."

"Of all the damn things, my Afghan hound was picked up by the dog-catcher and I have to go down to the dog pound to claim him."

"There's an emergency village ordinance protest meeting being called tonight and I have to be there because I'm on the block committee."

If you want to avoid wasting another evening with a bore . . .

The next time he calls to invite you over, reply at once: "The 10th? Great, I'll mark it down . . . (*Long pause*) . . . Uh-oh, I'm sorry, but that's the night I promised to join the Favershams for dinner."*

If you *anticipate* the bore's call . . .

Answer the phone without saying hello. Then mimic

---

* You might also have such "previous appointments" as a theatre date, a lodge meeting, or a moonlighting job. Just make sure the caller can't check up on you.

the bloodless tone of a tape recording and say: "This is an electronic recording. Mr. Jones is away. Please dictate your message when you hear the bell ..." *(Have a glass handy, and rap it with a teaspoon for a bell-like effect ... Place your hand over the mouthpiece and count out one minute ... then hang up.)*

If the bore gives you a long list of dates to choose from...

Give him this contemporary cop-out guaranteed to keep him off your back for an indefinite period: "I'll level with you, Merv. I've signed up for sensitivity training and can socialize only with my group until the shrink changes the rules. I'll let you know when that happens."

You can get out of going anywhere—a party, a luncheon, a meeting—by lying: "I have to go to the doctor." But even though that alibi may get you out of going, it isn't convincing. It's trite, cliché, and open to suspicion. Give it a twist. Be original, creative, imaginative.

The secret? *Be specific!*

For example ...

"I have to see my doctor about a vasectomy."

"I have to go to the doctor for an intravenous pyelogram."

"I have an appointment at my doctor's for a G.I. series."

"I have to deliver my wife's urine specimen to my doctor for a rabbit test."

"I have to go to the doctor for my allergy shots."

"I have a date with my doctor. He wants to tape my knee."*

Around the world with clever alibis

You've been talking up a storm about your upcoming cruise to the Caribbean. One day you get a phone call from another couple who tell you the cruise sounds so great they'd like to join you. But you're not looking for company, especially *their* company.

How do you discourage them from booking passage?

Shuck 'em with this shocker: "Am I glad you called us before you called your travel agent! Forget everything we said about this cruise. We just found out that it's almost booked solid by a crazy cult of hippies and we're trying to get our money back."

That should turn them off.

You kick off your high heels and settle back in your seat for the long train ride home. A huge, threatening

---

* If you're truly desperate, make this absolutely foolproof by wrapping a few yards of tape around one knee—so that the cynics can *feel* the evidence.

hulk of a man plumps himself down beside you and, ignoring the fact that it isn't the smoking car, pulls a big black cigar from his pocket. "You don't mind my smoking, do you?" he asks in a voice that dares you to say yes.

How do you make your answer mean yes without saying so?

Let *him* start worrying by telling him gently: "No, I don't mind your smoking—if you don't mind my getting sick."

Watch that cigar go back into his pocket.

It was a rat race getting to the airport and you just made the plane by the skin of your teeth. You sink gratefully into your seat beside a woman who smiles at you pleasantly. She's in the mood for conversation, but you aren't. You've a three-hour flight ahead of you and you just want to sit quietly and read the papers. But she begins chattering away. Ignoring her doesn't discourage her. You can't change your seat because every one is taken. You're her captive audience.

Is there any way out except through the emergency door?

Relax, friend, there is. Silence her with this stunner: "I know you're trying to tell me something, lady, but it's no use. You see, I'm stone deaf."

Up, up and away!

You've taken your family on one of those penny-pincher vacations in Nassau. You, the wife and your three kids are all shacked up in one room. But it's just your luck to have a neighbor from home check into the same hotel and spot your gang living like welfare guests. Are you embarrassed!

Well, you needn't be. Not if you greet the neighbor with this nifty: "Some joint this is! They screwed up our reservations and sardined us into this one room. We're lucky we aren't sleeping in the lobby!"*

You make an impulsive decision to fly to Miami for a warm winter weekend. But your travel agent informs you that all flights are filled.

Do not despair. Pack your luggage and take the public limousine to the airport. Then seek out an executive and sock it to him with this heart-rending romantic alibi: "I have to get back for my wedding. If I don't get to Miami by tonight my girl will be waiting at the church tomorrow morning!"

Remember, almost every flight keeps a seat or two available for VIPs who may show up at the last minute.

And, because all the world loves a lover, the airline exec will escalate you into an instant **VIP**.

For added credibility, we suggest you show him the ring for your phantom bride . . . which you purchased an hour ago at Woolworth's.

Everyone in your social circle but you has been abroad. To offset the effect on your social standing, you

---

* This is much more convincing that the oldie: "Who needs a fancy room? We spend all our time on the beach anyway."

noise it around that you're going to see the world during your upcoming vacation. But when the time comes to make good your boast, everything goes wrong: a big business deal falls through, your stocks drop, and a hefty promissory note falls due. You're too short of funds to do anything except freeload at your in-laws' cottage in the Catskills. If your friends find out, you'll be treated like a pariah.

Fear not, friend. We have a continental cop-out for you that'll let you go to the Catskills on the cuff and return home a world traveler. Just do these two things: 1) While away, read a guidebook on the countries of your choice so that you can sling the bull like a real tourist. 2) Before coming home, visit the gift shop of a large museum that sells authentic handmade items imported from around the world. Purchase a variety of such trinkets, wrapping each one differently, and present them to your friends as souvenirs of your world tour.*

If anyone asks why you didn't send postcards from abroad, just say: "The tour escort told us not to bother because the mails are so slow we'd be home before the postcards."

The only way you and your wife could manage a trip to Paris financially was to cut corners at every turn. You're stopping at a fleabag hotel on the outskirts of the

* No less a world traveler than *The New York Times* art critic John Canaday has adapted this high adventure hoax to his own ends, admitting: "I have selected many a wedding and graduation present, fostering the deception that I picked them up for the lucky recipients in my travels to exotic places."

city. One day you step out of the lobby and run smack into some hometown acquaintances who are in the area slumming. Very shocked, they say to you, "Is *this* where you're staying?"

Time again to think positive. Very self-assuredly, reply: "Of course. Where else can you meet the common people?"

After all, that's what *they* dropped by for.

Put-ons and put-downs

An alibi can be snappy, hokey, inane, logical, cruel, elaborate, disdainful or whatever. An evasion can often be as effective as a carefully reasoned argument. The only test of a good alibi is its result. Does it get you off the spot? You'll know if you get a nod of agreement, a chuckle, a gesture of helplessness, and the subject is dropped.

The whirlwind alibi often takes the form of a put-on or put-down. Here are a few examples:

You throw a lavish Bar Mitzvah, far beyond your means, for your thirteen-year-old son. When a guest asks how you can afford such a resplendent affair, you shrug, "Listen, if I couldn't afford it, would I do it?"

You're a gal in your thirties and still single. One of those snippety young mothers with razors in her mouth cuts you down with, "How come a pretty girl like you hasn't married?"

Slash her right back with, "I didn't have to."

You take your girl out for a ride and put one arm around her while you're driving. "As a favor to me," she pleads, "will you please use both hands?"

Give that cutie this cutie: "I wish I could, but I have to steer with one."

Every day, the same professional panhandler works your street and hands you the same weary line. And every day you stiff him. But he keeps coming back singing the same old tune: "Excuse me, sir, would you give me a quarter for a cup of coffee?"

Give him the finalizer, very sincerely: "I would, my good man, but I never drink coffee."

You hired a glamor girl for a secretary but, to protect your domestic tranquility, described her quite differently to your frau. Now, as you foresaw, she drops in on you without notice, takes a gander at the glamor puss and snaps, "I thought you told me your new secretary was at least forty!"

Give her the benefit of your foresight: "I was referring to her bust measure."

A busybody learns that you and your husband aren't getting along together. When she meets you on the street, she has the unmitigated nerve to ask you, "If you aren't happy, why don't you get a divorce?"

Don't just tell her to mind her own business. Eye her with disdain and declare: "If you must know, we're staying together on account of the children. Louie won't take 'em and I won't take 'em!"

You had a rip-roaring argument with a fellow member at the regular PTA meeting. The next day you find a letter in your mailbox with just one word written on it: "Stupid!" You know who it's from, and you can't let it go unchallenged.

Carve up the culprit at the next PTA meeting by holding up the letter and declaiming: "I found this in my mailbox after last week's meeting. Believe me, I've received many letters from people who forgot to sign their name. But this is the first instance I know of someone signing his name and forgetting to write the letter!"

Look "Stupid" squarely in the eye and watch him squirm!

The gang is making still another collection at the office, this time for a guy who broke his leg and will be out for a month. You've been hit for donations so often you've had to skimp on your lunches. Still, you'd shell out, except for the all-important fact that you hate this particular guy and secretly hope he breaks the other leg while trying to stand up on this one.

How are you going to get out of kicking in?

The answer, my friend, is—protest and pretend: "Uh-uh . . . count me out this time. I want to send him something personally."

A poison-pen letter, perchance?

The female shopper

If you're the average woman, this has happened to you. You're in a shoe store and have tried on more than a dozen pairs of shoes. But you find something wrong with all of them. The salesman is about to throw a tantrum and you're becoming very much embarrassed, feeling obligated to buy.

You don't have to buy. There's a way out. Tell the salesman, "My feet hurt from trying on so many shoes I can't tell what fits and what doesn't. I'll soak them tonight and come back tomorrow."

Then clear out of there.

You buy a good dress you've been admiring in the store window all week. After wearing it to a wedding, you decide to return it because it's not an everyday dress and the next big affair is years away. So you pack it neatly in its original box and tell the salesgirl that your husband doesn't like it and you want your money back. She asks if you wore it. Of course you say no. Then she says, "How come there are perspiration stains around the armpits?"

Don't sputter. Get indignant: "Look at that . . . so I'm not the *first* to return this dress!"

If she puts you on to the store manager, don't mince words telling him how shocked you are to have been sold used merchandise. Put a little muscle in your protest and threaten to report the store to the Board of Health.

A dress shop in town is holding a progressive discount sale: 20 per cent off each week until the discount reaches 80 per cent of the original price. By that time, though, most of the choice items will have been snapped up. Well, you walk in the first day of the sale, select a dress priced at $100 and deduct the full 80 per cent. When you hand the clerk your check for $20, he smirks, "Madam, this dress won't sell for that price until four weeks from now."

Very patiently, explain: "I know. That's why I post-dated the check."

It's logical.

A friend takes you shopping in a gourmet shop where prices are so high that if you spend a dollar, they ring up

NO SALE! This doesn't faze your wealthy friend. She purchases delicacy after delicacy. The temptation to follow suit is unbearable but your pocketbook won't take it. Your friend looks at you quizzically: "Don't you see *anything* here that tempts you?"

Tell her: "Everything. My eyes say yes, but my ulcer says no. It's all so irresistible, though, I'll take some homemade pot cheese and sesame crackers just for a snack."

You saved your money—and your pride.

You drive to town to do some shopping but can't find parking space. Fed up with hunting, you pull into the private lot behind the bank marked: "Parking for Savings Bank Customers Only. Show Pass Book for Validation."

Later, when you come to claim your car—your arms loaded with packages—the vigilant attendant demands: "Show me your pass bankbook."

Don't try to get away with telling him you can't get a hand free to reach into your purse. He'll never buy that. But here's one he will buy.

Very politely, tell him: "I wanted to get something from my vault. But when I got into the bank, I discovered that I'd left my vault key at home. Anyway, so that my trip shouldn't be a total loss, I stopped at a store a few doors away to pick up some things I'd ordered."

This original excuse should quell his suspicion, and you're home free!

Social bloopers

The wise alibi artist knows that the shortest distance between two points of view is a crooked line. Always keep this in mind when you put your foot in your mouth. Take, as an example, your yen to make it with the "in" crowd. So you brag about seeing the Broadway smash musical, *No, No, Nanette*, piling it on with: "I had two on the aisle last night, and you know how tough it is to get even bad seats for that hit!"

So far, so good. Then someone asks about the star: "Was Ruby Keeler good?"

"Good?" you exclaim. "She got a standing ovation and took nine curtain calls!"

That's when somebody else pipes up: "How strange. I read in a gossip column that she was sick and her understudy took over."

The only thing for you to do is tread a crooked line with the Back-Track Alibi. You say, "Impossible. Ruby Keeler was on stage last Saturday night."

Naturally the other guy is going to reply, "I thought you said *last night*?"

Your humble retort: "Either you misunderstood me or I made a mistake. I meant last Saturday night."

Now take your foot out of your mouth.

All the smart crowd is attending a big cocktail party and, to your great delight, you're invited. It's another rung up on your climb to fame and fortune. The joint is jammed with everybody who's anybody. You spot a very dapper gent across the room whose very presence makes needles rise on your skin. This guy took you but good in a business deal. Just seeing him makes you so angry you have to spill out your feelings to someone. So you turn to the unfamiliar but attractive woman sipping a Scotch beside you and mutter, "I *hate* that guy!"

In a shocked voice, she exclaims, "Why, that's my husband!"

At that moment you need an alibi like a man in an iron lung needs oxygen. Be glad you bought this book—here's your alibi. Leer a little at the lady and say: "I know, Beautiful—*that's* why I *hate* him."

The look she gives you will guarantee that you made her evening. In fact, don't be surprised if she offers you her phone number.

A VIP with an appliance manufacturing firm did you a big favor by obtaining a freezer for you at cost. You're so elated that you brag to everybody about your great connections and the tremendous deal you got. Now a friend wants you to get a freezer for him.

How are you going to get out of this without blowing the friendship?

Give him the just-between-you-and-me treatment, like this: "Don't spread this around, Leon, but I just found out the guy I bought it from is a fence. The D.A.'s investigating him. When he told me the freezer was a steal, it *was*."

You'll keep the friend. Nobody wants a hot freezer.

It's intermission time at the theatre and you make for the lobby to grab a quick smoke. Out of the crowd comes a woman you haven't seen in ten years (and would be happy if you didn't see for another ten), screaming, "Paul!"

For the life of you, you can't recall her name. She feels crushed and says, "I'm Thelma Rudnick! We met at the Matalons in Jamaica. How could you forget?"

More important—how can you extricate yourself from this social goof?

All it takes is that magic combination of chutzpah and warmth: "Thelma! I would never have recognized you—you look so much *younger!*"

You're having some of the girls in for a good-natured game of canasta and there just isn't room for cantankerous Clara. Better be prepared, though, with a good reason why you left her out, before she asks you why.

We recommend that soon after the party, you telephone her to ask if she's feeling any better. Naturally, she'll wonder what in blazes you're talking about—since she wasn't sick in the first place.

That's your cue to act surprised and say: "Oh, Clara,

I'd heard you were feeling terrible and assumed your allergies* were acting up. That's why I didn't bother you to come in to the canasta game this afternoon."

She'll be sufficiently impressed by your solicitude to forgive and forget. If she does ask who told you she was feeling rotten, beg off with: "Gee, I don't remember, one of the girls, I guess."

You like your beauty parlor, but you hear that the new operator is better than your regular hairdresser. Switching operators, however, presents quite a problem, as you girls know. If you haven't reached the exalted rank of SHAM,† you'll never be able to think of a usable alibi. Well, we have a suggestion.

Phone the beauty parlor for an appointment—not for yourself, but for a friend, and say that she wants to try the new hairdresser, Alfred. When it comes time for her appointment, *you* show up instead, alibiing, "Mrs. Carter came down with a virus this morning and couldn't keep her appointment. I volunteered to take her place so that Alfred shouldn't have to lose a customer."

That will get you off the hook with your regular operator. If you like Alfred and want to use him again, you can request him on this pretext: "He changed my hair style and it's his responsibility to correct it."

* If she doesn't have allergies, hang it on some other chronic ailment she complains about, anything from headaches to arthritis. Everyone has *something*.
† Sure-Handed Alibi Master.

After a second visit to Alfred, your old operator will think you're stuck with Alfred and be glad.

You don't quite catch the name of someone to whom you've just been introduced, and you're ashamed to ask him to repeat it.

You don't have to. Just say: "Do you spell your name with an 'e' or an 'i'?"

Nine out of ten names will have one of those letters in it. But whether it does or not, he'll spell it out for you. Get it right this time.

You picked up an old vase at a rummage sale. One evening you have some friends over for a visit. When one of your guests admires the vase, you tell her it's a valuable antique. She startles you by saying: "I'd swear it was the same vase I contributed to the local rummage sale."

Do you have an answer?

We have one for you. Just smile and say: "Really? I've picked up some of my most valuable things at rummage sales. This vase is worth a small fortune."

That should leave her guessing.

You've been asked to judge a beauty contest. One of the entrants is your friend's daughter, but another is a gal on whom you have designs. Naturally, you cast your vote for the latter—on a favor-for-favor basis. You figure no one will ever find out because it's a secret ballot. However, another judge who coveted the same broad learns how you voted and gives you away. Your friend's daughter passes the word to her dad.

How can you explain your not voting for his daughter?

Let him in on the "secret" of what goes on behind the scenes in beauty contests by saying: "You ought to be grateful to me. To win a crown, a girl has to agree to make a nudie picture and be manhandled by a bunch of perverts!"

You can document this alibi by giving the guy a copy of the best-seller, *The Contest*.

The family has enjoyed a fine dinner at a fine restaurant but there's a lot of steak left on their plates. Always the thrifty one, you tell the waiter, "Please put those bones in a bag. We want to take them home for the dog."

Your precocious eight-year old zaps you with: "But, daddy, we don't have a dog."

Grin at the child through grated teeth and grunt: "I know, son, but Mr. Brown next door does!"

P.S.: Leave a nice tip.

A friend of yours gives you a painting she did herself. It's awful, and you hide it behind the piano, hanging it up only when she visits you. But one day she drops in without notice and leaves you no time to put up her painting. Even worse, she spies it sticking out from behind the piano.

Don't apologize profusely. Alibi shamelessly: "I'm having some redecorating done and there'll be workmen in and out of here all day. So if you noticed, I hid your wonderful painting behind the piano for safe-keeping because I don't want it stolen or scratched."

With that alibi, you might even get another painting.

Sequel: It might happen that your friend will drop by again just as unexpectedly a few days later—and will again see her painting hidden, but nothing changed in the room. What do you say when she asks: "What work did you have done?"

You simply answer with a sigh: "Nothing yet. You know the labor market, nobody shows up. It's always tomorrow, and I'm still waiting."

Swellhead you are, but egghead you aren't. Nevertheless, in your eagerness to impress some new acquaintances at a party, you rattle off the titles of some heavyweight books of social commentary—none of which you've read. The closest you've gotten to them is through a brief review or two. Now to your great dismay, a *true* egghead who has read one of these books from cover to cover asks you about a specific point in a significant passage.

You blundered into this mess. How do you blunder out?

With the blunderbuss alibi! Lunge right in with this

reply: "Well, that's a big question. It isn't anything I care to be *simplistic* about because this has to do with the *main thrust* of the *thesis*. Any *viable explanation* has to go beyond the *ad hoc principle* at issue. Do I make myself clear?"*

That'll shut him up.

As a special service to our readers, we present our Save-A-Friend department. Here you are in the beauty parlor busily gossiping about a mutual acquaintance. The conversation is distinctly unfavorable to the third party. Suddenly a head pops out of the hair dryer opposite you. It belongs to the gal you've been panning, and you can see that she overheard everything!

How do you save a friend?

Give her the mind-boggling Q.R.A.† Look her straight in the eye and say, "Ha! We were wondering when you'd begin to notice we were here!"

That should turn the tables in your favor. But be prepared for the possibility that she might be unusually foxy

---

* You can juggle this jargon around any way you like. Commit to memory some of the key words printed here in italics. Sprinkle them liberally in your conversation. Here are some more egghead words to jot down for future reference, and very useful in high IQ society:

> *ambiance*
> *pejorative*
> *cinema verité*
> *redundant*
> *pragmatic*

† Quick Recovery Alibi.

and press the issue, asking, "Then why didn't you say something *nice* about me?"

How are you going to top yourself?

Simply snap back: "If we did, you'd *never* come out!"

When you say that, you touch a nerve. No female would dare contradict you.

How to look a gifthorse in the face

When it comes to giving or getting gifts, alibis are a must. The wise alibi artist is way ahead of the game, always thoughtful and considerate. Here are some examples for a variety of awkward situations.

You bring some friends a gift of table linens that you purchased at a discount store, but rewrapped in a Saks Fifth Avenue box. When they open the box, the wife exclaims: "Oh, they're beautiful!" She pauses a few seconds, then adds: "But they're red and our decor is green. Would you be offended if we exchanged them for a green set?"

You don't mind at all—except that you know that they'll be taking them back to the wrong store. And if *you* insist on returning them yourself, it's very likely that *they* will refuse to let you go to all that trouble. You have to come up with a far better answer.

Here's your alibi: "You don't want red? Oh, how lucky for *us*! To be perfectly honest, we've been hunting everywhere for a set like this in red for ourselves. Please don't return it. Let us keep it, and we'll get *you* a set in green."

Now they can't protest.

A friend gave you a piece of bric-a-brac so hideous looking that you passed it off on someone lacking taste enough to know good from bad. But now this friend pays you a visit and peers everywhere to see where you've displayed her gift. You know from her hurt look that you have to come up with a considerate alibi.

Do you have one?

If you don't, we do. Just tell her: "You know that lovely piece you gave me? Well, my niece visited me and simply fell in love with it. I just had to let her have it."

Your friend won't take offense; she'll feel flattered.

On the other hand, this could happen . . .

You take your friend's gift back to the store where she bought it, hoping to exchange it for something more appropriate. But who comes along and catches you in the act? That very same friend!

How are you going to get out of this embarrassing bind?

Nothing to it if you think fast (or crib from this book). As soon as she spots you, brighten up and exclaim: "Look, someone else gave me the very same lovely gift you did. So I'm keeping *yours* and exchanging *hers*."

She has to believe you because she can't prove otherwise.

An old school chum from out-of-town drops in on you one afternoon, bringing you a piece of pop-art sculpture as a gift. You admire it to be polite and set it on the mantle. When your husband arrives home from work, the first remark out of the big boob's mouth is: "Where'd you get that horrible looking hunk of junk?"

What do you say to your embarrassed friend who's still waiting to be introduced to Mr. Big Mouth?

Your best bet is to bring him down with this belittler: "Now I know it's a masterpiece. My husband's idea of art is the centerfold of Playboy!"

That kind of private joke at his expense will ease your guest's embarrassment—and yours as well.

You pick up a gift at a bargain price in a special sale. You have it gift-wrapped and present it to a friend. But when the package is opened and the gift taken out, you're embarrassed to see the price tag still on it—marked down!

Don't blush. Just breeze your way out with this beaut.

Very boldly, say: "Can I please have that tag? I'm furious at that store. There was a sale going on but they told me this item *wasn't* marked down and made me pay the full price!"

Mark our words—your friend will fall for this marked-down alibi.

In your hall closet you have stashed away a large collection of gifts that were given to you by house guests over the years. These showy but useless trinkets provide you with a treasure trove into which you dip when you need a little gift for some occasion. Now you've been invited to a dinner party and you choose a nice set of coasters, wrap them prettily and present them to your hostess. When she unwraps the package, she says with a twinge of sarcasm: "How thoughtful of you to bring the same coasters *I* brought *you* six months ago."

A deadly coincidence! But instead of blushing, strike back with this speedy stratagem. "We liked them so much we wanted you to have a set, too. Those are exact duplicates of the ones you brought us."

She may be skeptical,* but she'll always have that nagging doubt that will force her to accept your explanation.

Have you ever gone to a party where everyone but you has brought a gift?

---

* You can remove the last shred of skepticism by buying a set of identical coasters for yourself and using them on her next visit to your home.

Here are some extricators *par excellence:*

1) "We bought you a nice cake but I sat on it getting out of the car and we had to dump it."

2) "We wanted to see what everyone else brought so that we wouldn't duplicate somebody else's gift."

3) "John thought *I* had it, I thought *he* had it, and now we find your gift is still at home!"

Survival kit of one-shot alibis

No Alibible would be complete without a selection of gilt-edged alibis for all occasions. We call these One-Shot Alibis because one serves many purposes. We suggest you burn them into your memory for instant use when you're up against the wall and can't get unpinned. Here are some examples you can try out at your next party.

What do you say to someone who asks:
    "Why won't you check into a motel with me?"
    "How come you didn't send out Christmas cards?"
    "Why can't you ever sneak out on your wife?"
    "If you're so worried about accidents, why not get a vasectomy?"
One alibi is all you need: *"It's against my religion."*

And store this one away for future reference . . .

What's your reply to these queries:

"How come you don't open a charge account at that new department store branch?"

"Whatsa matter you won't sign my promissory note?"

"Is there some reason you don't carry cash?"

"Why don't you hire a painter instead of doing it yourself?"

The everything alibi: *"I'd be breaking a New Year's resolution."*

Here's another you can rely on . . .

How do you answer questions like these:

"Were you a virgin when you were married?"

"What did you pay for that dress?"

"Do you ever cheat?"

"How often do you have sex?"

"Are you Jewish?"

The one-shot retort: *"If you can't tell, what's the difference?"*

And add this trusty tidbit to your alibi arsenal . . .

How do you brush off these posers:

"Why don't you take a trip to Europe?"

"What's the reason you don't play the market any more?"

"Why have you avoided marriage?"

"If you don't like the neighborhood, why not move elsewhere?"

"How come you quit dieting?"

A single alibi will do: *"It's bad for my condition!"*

What would you say if you're seen at the neighborhood bar when you're supposed to be on the wagon?

Use this spunky copout: *"I just stopped by to use the bathroom."**

If you're in double jeopardy because you're trapped with a glass in your hand, top yourself with: "Well, I couldn't walk out without buying something!"

P.S. to Alibi Lovers: Sometimes One-Shot Alibis are interchangeable. Learn them all and be prepared for anything!

How to succeed in business by really lying

No man ever made it to the top who couldn't lie successfully. Good alibis are what keep business ethics separate from ordinary ethics. Master them and you'll be Mr. Big before you know it.

---

* You can also use this line whenever you're caught someplace you shouldn't be, as for instance:

At your broker's office watching the Big Board (when you swore off playing the market),

At the porno peepshow (when you have a rep as Mr. Respectable in your community),

At the Unemployment Insurance office (when you bragged how you'd never be laid off from your job).

You were overlooked for a big promotion after having bragged to everyone about getting a vice-presidency. Now you have to weasel out.

Here's your weasel: "It was too much of a sacrifice. I'd have had to give up my family life and practically sleep with the company."

There's a firm that owes you and almost everybody else in town money. Well, we have a sure-fire fib to make him pay up.

Scare the daylights (and the cash) out of him by saying, "Unless I get your check by next Monday, I'll tell all your other creditors that you paid *us*!"

He'll pay you fast to keep the others off his back.

One alibi may not be enough. A deteriorating situation can get you in deeper and deeper, as for instance . . .

A few weeks ago you let a guy in on something sensational: a very astutely planned coup on Wall Street. Unifax Ltd., which could be had then at 62, was ready to take off and go straight up. But now, on the day you run into the guy, it is selling (after a recent rally) at 23. He says to you, "What the hell happened to that coup?"

Remain cool and calm, and confide with a sly wink: "The S.E.C. got wind of it, so the big boys are throwing them off the trail."

That should hold him—for a while.

P.S.: When the stock goes down to 11, re-assure him: "I'm

putting every cent I have into it. If it was a solid buy at 62—*and believe me, it was*—just think what a bargain it is at 11."

P.P.S.: If it goes any lower, your next alibi should be mailed from Ethiopia where you have recently moved (we hope).

Your insurance agent calls you up to renew your policy. But you want to cancel the account because you can get a better deal from someone else.

Is there a painless way to do the deed?

There is. We call it the Benign Break-off. Make it short, sweet, and sincere: "Listen, Ed, I hate to do this to an old buddy but I have to cancel my account. My boss' son has just gone into the business and, you know, nepotism knows no bounds."*

He'll understand. He knows what nepotism means because he himself probably started out by collaring his kin as clients.

That eager young beaver in your office has been bucking you, the boss, for a raise. How do you stall him without making him want to join the picket line?

This way: "Son, I can't afford to give you even a nickel raise. But I wouldn't sell you for a million dollars!"

That's telling him he's worth his weight in gold—but you keep the gold.

How to Wheel-and-Deal...

---

* The Benign Break-off can likewise be adapted to sever ties with your stockbroker, lawyer, or accountant.

You want to order some supplies for your small firm but can't afford to put up the cash. Since your credit is no longer good at the ABC Company, you have to find another supplier.

The First Step: Telephone their competitor, the XYZ Company, and address them in the authoritative manner of a big business tycoon, getting right to the point, and saying, "This is Mr. Clobber of the Clobber Corporation and we'd like to place an order with you people. We used to deal exclusively with the ABC Company but found them slow and undependable. I've heard that your firm is more reliable."

You'll have the XYZ Company eating out of your hand. As soon as you receive your first shipment—but before you get billed—place another big order. Within a few weeks, be prepared to get a call from an XYZ executive gingerly asking for money.

The Second Step: Stall off paying as long as possible. For this, you need a repertoire of cheeky chicanery. From the following list, pick whichever best fits your mood as a starter, then use the rest to stretch your credit to the breaking point.

The Instant Respect Ploy: "Confidentially, our firm is going public, and all our outflowing cash entries are frozen until we register with the SEC." (He'll probably beg you to let him buy some stock at the issue price.)

The Belittler: "Listen, all small bills like yours, under $10,000, are handled by our outside accountant. And he won't be back from Europe until the end of the month. I'll see that he gives you priority."

The Busy Technique: "Can't talk now. I'm just about to grab the company plane to negotiate a merger with one of our biggest competitors."

The Nixon Alibi: "We're being investigated by a team from the president's price-freeze department, and they want to go over every one of your bills. So will you please send us Xeroxes of your prices on the stuff we ordered from you pre-September 1st?"

The Obvious (and Best) Alibi: "The fettucini has hit the fan, pal. Our computer blew out and we're three weeks behind on everything."

The Twisteroo: "We've held up on your bill because our bookkeeper thinks you undercharged yourself. Will you please review your entire bill in detail and see if you cheated yourself?"

The Third Step: Pay up, or hijack a plane to Cuba.

In order to beat the high cost of living, you have your wife working as your secretary. But you don't want any of the people you do business with to know the *real* reason why you haven't hired someone. That would make you look hungry, and that would hurt business.

So how will you explain your wife's working for you?

Take your pick of alibis . . .

1) "Now I don't have to take my business home with me nights."

2) "I'm a terror to work for. She's the only woman who can put up with me."

3) "She's ten times better than anyone I've ever hired."

4) "My psychiatrist said it would be a great way to enrich our relationship. And you know something? It has!"

Have you ever reached the point-of-no-return with a salesman? He's been pitching and you've been listening, tacitly encouraging him until you get to the point where you can't easily turn him down.

Ah, but now you can because we've dreamed up a doozy for you. It works on all kinds of pitchmen from real estate salesmen to insurance agents, and from stock brokers to exterminators. When you want to call off the deal, just phone the pitchman and say: "Listen, it's a whole new ball game. My wife and I just split up, so we won't be needing that cottage."*

The foxy art of ping-ponging

You can frustrate creditors and discourage busybodies with an alibi technique we call Ping-Ponging. Just bounce the nuisance back and forth like a ping-pong ball. Here are the two basic approaches . . .

* Or that speedboat, or that new policy, or whatever goods or services were being negotiated . . . except stuff marked His & Hers.

1) Person-to-Person Ping-Ponging

You're a businessman without enough ready cash on hand to meet your bills. But because you have a partner, you can Ping-Pong when a creditor makes a dunning phone call to you.

Tell him: "Frank (your partner) is taking care of it."

When Frank gets the creditor's call, his reply is: "Sam (that's you) is handling your account."

When the creditor comes back to you, say: "I *used* to handle your account. Now Frank's in charge."

When he goes back to Frank, he just says: "This isn't new business. Take it up with Sam, he's on top of it."

As the alibis go bouncing back and forth, the creditor experiences exasperation—and you buy time.

2) Place-to-Place Ping-Ponging

Your friend wants to borrow your good evening gown to wear to an upcoming wedding. You don't want to lend it to her because you know she'll stretch it out of shape. Naturally, you wouldn't dream of telling her that. The only alternative to such an insult would be a flat refusal, but that would also be an insult. You need an alibi that will stretch out over a period of time. The solution is to Ping-Pong.

When she makes her first request for the gown, tell her, "Oh, it's at the cleaner's."

A few days later, when she calls again, say, "I have to wear it to a dinner party Sunday. Try me next week."

Next week, tell her, "A seam ripped and my mother is fixing it on her sewing machine."

If she still hasn't gotten the message, and calls again, say, "Mother fixed it but dropped it off at my office when she was in town."

On her next call, if she's still holding out, tell her, "Oh, the stupid steno took the package home with her by mistake."

By this time, the wedding will probably have come and gone. If not, just Ping-Pong until it has . . . right up to the Great Wall of China.

How to lie to the family, in-laws and relatives

Alibis are a necessity to keep members of a family on speaking terms. Let's say that your mother-in-law has just served you a meal for the first time at a family get-together. She wants to know what you thought of it.

Since you didn't think much of it, you simply tell her, "The soup was cold, the roast was tough and the gravy was bitter. But, mom, that's *just* the way I like it!"

In this way, you keep your dignity intact, your relationship intact, but your mother-in-law will get the message. On your next visit, the soup will be hot, the roast tenderized, and the gravy sweetened. Then, when she asks you how you like the meal, you can say, "It's even better than the last one!"

Here's a case where you have a brother-in-law in the insurance business. You don't want to buy a policy from him because you've committed your business elsewhere.

You just say to him confidentially, "Joe, don't tell your sister, but I have a weak heart and can't pass the medical examination."

You made the mistake of wearing the same gown to this wedding that you wore to one a month ago. It doesn't go unnoticed by an eagle-eyed cousin who's a bit of a snob. She looks you over and says, "Oh, didn't you wear that to the last affair?"

She deserves a slap in the face, but if that's not your style, gush right back: "Yes, dear. I'm superstitious, you see, and I *always* wear this gown to weddings to bring good luck to the bride and groom."

You're entitled.

After being married only a few short months, you and your husband are invited to a large family gathering. A distant cousin whom you hardly know, even by name, asks, "Did you like the toaster we sent you for a wedding present?"

You received three toasters and can't remember who sent what. Not wishing to offend the cousin, you put on an appreciative smile and alibi, "Oh yes, the toaster is just lovely."

Your cousin grimaces and says, "Excuse me, I made a mistake. We sent you a clock."

Did she really make a mistake, or did she try to trip you up because you neglected to send a thank-you note? You aren't sure, but in any case you goofed. Here's how to ungoof yourself. Say coolly, "I know, cousin, but I didn't want to embarrass you."

Now just suppose that the cousin doesn't let things end there but comes back with a biting, "I'm surprised we didn't hear from you. We were worried that you hadn't received it."

She may think she has you. Not quite. Just tell her, "Oh, we're still waiting for the thank-you notes to arrive from the printer's. He got our order all messed up."

Give that alibi the touch of authenticity when you get home by dropping that relentless relative a hand-written note saying, "The engraved thank-you notes still haven't arrived, so we're writing you personally to say thanks."

Your youngster is doing his homework and doesn't know the answer to a question. He puts it to you but you don't know it, either.

Do you have to admit your ignorance?

Not on your life. Put the kid on his own with this slick sally: "Hey, that's a tricky one. Take another fifteen minutes to figure it out for yourself. If you do, I'll give you a quarter. If you don't, I'll give you the answer."

That should give you enough time to call up someone for the answer and make like a genius.

It's Saturday afternoon. Your mother-in-law phones and says she'd like to come over and spend the evening with you. But you're having some friends in and would prefer that she didn't come around. So you tell her, "Gee, mom, you'd better not. The whole family must have come down with a virus. We're all feeling lousy."

Later that night when the party's in full swing, the doorbell rings. It's your mother-in-law—with a kettle of chicken soup!

How are you going to get out of this booboo?

Don't chicken out. Give her a big greeting: "I knew it! Why is it I have to make out someone's sick for you to make us chicken soup?"

Then ladle out a bowl of Jewish penicillin to each guest to celebrate your quick recovery. She'll love the whole scene.

A friend gave you some marijuana and you decide to try a few puffs in the safety of your living room. But your teenage son comes home from school unexpectedly early, barges right in and catches you in the middle of a big drag on the joint. He's smelled enough grass around the school to know what you're smoking.

Does this mean the end of his respect for you as a parent?

Not if you use this tactical maneuver. Start coughing and complain, "Oh, this is awful stuff! The PTA asked all the parents to try pot so they could deal with the problem more realistically. I'm sorry I volunteered."

His respect for your spirit of adventure will be monumental.

The bank makes an error in your favor and you have no intention of calling their attention to it. The windfall makes for great conversation at the family dinner table. Suddenly, however, your youngster pipes up, asking: "Why don't you return the money?"

It's a perfect opening for a pious put-down. Very sternly, say: "People must learn to pay for their mistakes, my son."

Touché! You've converted an alibi into a moral lesson—a major triumph.

One of your get-rich-quick relatives wants you to invest in a very iffy proposition. Naturally, you want no part of this deal.

How do you cop out without creating a family scandal?

Shut him out with this shrewdie: "Sounds like a good deal, Morris, but you'll have to count me out. I was in partnership with a guy and he slapped me with a judgment. Now all my assets are frozen until the case comes up in court."

That'll freeze him out.

Small fry only: Kiddie Kop-outs . . .

This six-year-old is showing off his baseball talent to his uncle. He's promised him a dollar if he could prove he's a really good ballplayer.

The youngster tosses a ball up in the air, swings with his bat and misses. "That was just for practice," he alibis. Again he throws up the ball, swings and misses. "It's the third strike that counts," he alibis again. Once more he tosses up the ball, swings and misses. Then he claims the dollar.

"But you struck out," protests the uncle.

"Sure," says the kid. "That's because I'm such a great pitcher!"*

The child is on his way to becoming a Grand Master of the Alibi.

Your uncle gives you a dollar, assuming that you'll put it in the bank. But a few minutes later, he sees you on the street munching on pizza, soda pop and ice cream. "So

---

* This is the style of the progressive alibi, with one piling up on top of the other, ultimately paying off in a Grand Slam Zonker.

that's what you did with the dollar," he exclaims. "You spent it all on frivolities!"

Pacify him with this poignant plea: "When I *haven't* any money, I can't spend it. When I *have* money, I can't spend it. So when *can* I spend it?"

That'll stump him.

Your mother looks over your report card and asks: "Why did you get a failing mark in English composition?"

Make mom happy with the perfect alibi: 'Well, mom, the subject was 'The Trouble with Parents.' I had to write about all the things my parents do that turn me off and I couldn't think of even one."

Be ready for the biggest hug of your life.

Attention All Kids: Tear these next few alibis out of the book before your father spots them!

You promised to study your lessons and not watch TV. But your dad comes into your room, touches the set and finds it's hot. "So you *were* watching TV!" he exclaims accusingly. "And don't lie about it because I *know*—the set's still hot."

You don't have to lie. Just be "reasonable" and say: "Sure it was on, dad, but I wasn't watching it. Just like when mom says no matter what she has on, you never notice what she's wearing. Same thing with me—I didn't pay attention to what was on TV."

It's your round.

Despite your Dad's persistent warnings, you play ball on the front lawn. Then, one tragic afternoon, pow, wham—disaster! You've broken one of the windows in the front of the house. How to hustle Dad?

Grab the bull by the horns. When he comes home, after he has his dinner, approach him with quivering lips and say: "Dad, you know our big bay window in the parlor. Well, I was playing ball and . . . "

"You broke it?"

"No, Dad, not that one. The little one next to it."

He'll be so relieved life with father will be fairly tolerable that week.

You get into a name-calling contest with your creepy cousin who's visiting you. Mad as a hornet, you yell, "If you don't shut up, I'm gonna use a four-letter word!" Just then you hear your father's voice behind you say: "What four-letter word?"

Time for a Kiddie Kop-out: "Help."

Your dad has caught you fighting with the kid down the block. "I don't mind if you fight fair and square," he scolds you, "but I won't stand for you kicking anyone in the stomach, Why'd you do it?"

Stand your ground and say: "I didn't, dad. He just turned around too quick."

Remember—the child who can alibi is the man who can make it to the White House!

Adolescents only: High-school Hokum . . .

You bring home a terrible report card. Your father looks it over and groans, "How can a son of mine do so poorly!"

Be nonchalant and reply: "That's how it goes, dad. Nice guys always finish last."

You have an after-school job as a shipping clerk. One day your boss pops into the shipping department and finds you loafing in a corner with your feet up on a packing crate. He's boiling!

Cool him off with this sophisticated snapper. "Don't be upset, boss. This is the 34 minutes of each day that I'm working for the government."

Teenage alibi in two acts . . .

ACT ONE

After your boyfriend brings you home from a date,

you and he like to neck in his car parked outside your house. When your parents ask you why you never invite him in, what are you going to tell them?

We suggest this logical cop-out: "If I make him come in, he'll think I'm serious."

That should bridge the generation gap.

ACT TWO

You're necking hot and heavy when your highly moralistic maiden aunt comes by and catches you at it. What's your cop-out?

Don't look guilty. Brighten up. Push the guy away and say: "'Oh, auntie, I'm so glad you came by. Do you think our acting is realistic enough for the love scene in the school play?"

She'll quickly agree it is.

Co-ed Cop-out . . .

You come home from college during intersession dreading to inform your parents you failed a subject. The best way to break this unpleasant news is to precede it with even more unpleasant news.

Casually announce to your mother: "I'm in love with a wonderful guy, mom—but he's older than dad. And we're going to get married!" She'll all but faint. Then smile and say: "I was only kidding. But after that shock, you won't feel so bad when I tell you I flunked Chem."

This gambit is known as paving-the-way-with-a-lie.

We hope it doesn't happen often . . .

You're having a gay old time at the convention and are a little tipsy. Nature calls, and you navigate your way to the men's room—but it is really the ladies' lav. No sooner do you get comfortable than the door opens and a startled female stares pop-eyed down at you sitting at half-mast.

Denounce the indignation with this decimator: "Don't you think you're carrying this Women's Lib stuff a little too far?"

That should accelerate her exit and give you ten seconds to get away and sober up.

You're at the annual town barbecue and the local politicos are making speeches. When your favorite is introduced, you applaud him with gusto. But your gusto is short-lived when you spot your boss in the crowd and see him frowning disapprovingly. Obviously, he doesn't agree with your political views.

How do you appease his majesty?

Hold up your hands, clapping vigorously, and call out: "This is the only thing that helps my arthritis!"

He may be skeptical but he'll give you the benefit of the doubt.

You can't resist a visit to the new dirty book store

during your lunch hour. But when you come out, you run smack into one of the elders of your church.

Throw him off the track with this tall tale: "One of the college kids working at my place asked me to return a book for him. He was too ashamed to do it himself—and I don't blame him!"

You probably just provided the inspiration for next Sunday's sermon.

The whole town knows your grade school youngster got a public tongue-lashing from a local merchant when he caught the kid swiping a chocolate bar from his candy store. One of your wise-guy neighbors tells you: "If the kid's gonna steal, he should steal big—rob a bank!"

Take a tip from actor Bill Gargan and sock him with this squelcher: "He would have, but he doesn't get out of school till 3:30."

The wise guy won't bug you again.

You're one of those women who enjoy serving jury duty. Now at last you are called again. But when the clerk re-examines you, he says: "Madam, you put down the same age as you did when you served five years ago."

Draw back proudly and protest: "Well, naturally. I'm not one to say one thing today and another thing tomorrow!"

That's the kind of consistency that makes good jurors.

Big mouth that you are, you offer to fix a friend's TV set that isn't working well. After fiddling around with it a while, there's a puff of smoke and the whole set goes dead completely.

Turn the disaster into a stroke of good fortune by exclaiming: "Wow! It's a good thing that happened when I was around or you might have been electrocuted when you touched the dial!"

And be glad *you* didn't go up in a puff of smoke.

You're in your dentist's waiting room, reading a magazine while you await your turn. A recipe catches your eye, so you tear it out. But the nurse notices what you did.

Return her baleful stare with a smile and say: "I only want to borrow one page, so the other patients can enjoy the rest of the magazine."

Consideration takes many forms.

You think your golf partner is looking the other way, so you move the ball out of the sand trap. But you miscalculated. He spies you and calls out, "Hey, what are you up to?"

Get back in his good graces with this gasser: "Oh, I was only looking for a four-leaf clover to change my luck."

Don't dare try this gambit a second time.

You've just shed your shorts in your inamorata's apartment when you hear a key scrape in the front door lock. "My husband!" she gasps, shoving you into a walk-in closet along with your clothes. Seconds later you hear a man's voice say, "I'm going to change into my golf outfit." Suddenly the closet door swings open and the flabbergasted husband confronts you in the raw.

You'll have to scale the heights to get out of this jam. Seize the initiative at once and zonk him with the Mt. Everest in alibis: "I've been waiting in here out of respect for your wife. Now that you're home, let's talk business. I'm selling home-study courses for Masters and Johnson."

While you've got him with egg on his face, we suggest you throw on your coat and scram out of there fast!

The sports scene

Do you know how to be a good loser?

If you do, you have no need for alibis. But that, of course, is the wrong philosophy. Our purpose in writing this book is to make losers sound like winners, the only way to go. A reliable repertoire of zingy alibis can do it.

Take the field of sports . . .

It's Sunday afternoon and you get into a sandlot baseball game with some other fellows. You get up to bat and one-two-three strike out. A fellow team-mate, up next, razzes you, "Whatsa matter, can't you see the ball?"

"Shhh, I'm using psychology, you dope," is your reply. "I'm giving that pitcher false confidence and setting him up for you because you're a long ball hitter."

That puts *him* on the spot.

You decide to teach the neighborhood kids a thing or two about baseball. "The trick is to make the ball go where you want it to go," you say authoritatively, swinging a bat. "Throw me a pitch and I'll show you what I mean." You connect with the first pitch and the ball goes crrashing through a nearby window. The kids begin to giggle.

How are you going to regain your self-respect?

Simply wipe your brow and mutter: "Whew, that was a close one. I raised my bat just in time. If I'd have hit the grounder I was planning, the ball would have gone smack into that little old lady crossing the street!"

Put down the bat while you're still ahead. Of course, you'll have to pay for the broken window, but if your alibiing artistry runs true to form you'll blame it on some kid who can't hit straight.

These take chutzpah

There are special rewards for alibi artists with quick presence of mind and the ability to remain unrattled.* A good example is the Reverse Zinger—which is an alibi that proves itself coming and going.

* We call this talent *Alibi-ability*.

Your wife, helpful soul that she is, greets you at the
door and takes your jacket to hang it up in the closet. It
slips from her hands and when she picks it up, out of the
breast pocket fall two ticket stubs for *Oh! Calcutta!* To
make matters worse, they're dated for the night you
were supposed to be out bowling with the boys. No
longer the helpmate, she holds them out between pinched
fingers and demands, "What are these ticket stubs doing
in your suit pocket?"

Give her the Zinger. Feigning great relief, take the
stubs and say, "I've been looking everywhere for these.
Harvey Ruskin gave them to me so I could claim them as
entertainment expenses on my income tax return."

You're out in the clear—*unless she is cagier than you
think*. She might pursue the subject: "Why didn't Harvey
Ruskin use them for *his* income tax return?"

Time for the Reverse Zinger. Very virtuously, say,
"Because he told his wife he was bowling with us that
night."

You won the day.

Your youngster has a good time for himself splashing
around in the bathtub. But the water runs over the side,
seeps down to the apartment below and cracks the ceiling. Some water even dripped down and stained the fur-
niture. Both the landlord and the downstairs tenant are
furious. If you're stuck with the damages, it could run
into a lot of money.

You need a real biggie here. Get a wrench and open the water pipe in the bathroom just enough to allow the water to leak out profusely. Then call in the super and scream, "The damned pipes are leaking out a flood and I'm going to sue for damages!"

Make the landlord assume responsibility. He's insured, anyway.

You may not be the fastest gal on wheels but you're doing 65 mph on the turnpike which is 10 mph better than the posted speed limit. A casual glance in your rearview mirror warns you that a motorcycle cop is catching up to you. If he nabs you, you're almost sure to lose your driver's license because this will be your third major violation.

Should you slow down and try to sweet-talk the cop out of giving you a ticket?

That'll never work once he spots the violations on your license. Your only salvation is to outsmart the cop. Step on the gas. Push it up to 70, then 75, then 80 or more if necessary to keep in the lead, until you approach a service station. Pull up at once, park anywhere and race to the ladies' room. An irate motorcycle cop will be waiting for you when you come out.

Slip him your sweetest smile and say: "I'll bet you thought I'd never make it!"

You hail a cab at just about the same time as another

fellow. But he has the drop on you and reaches the taxi first. Even though you know he's more entitled, how do you get him to let you have the cab?

The way to do it is with the subtle intimidator. Mix defiance with politeness: "Sir, do you mind if I take this cab? If I'm forced to wait for another, I'll be late to my karate class."

He'll back down chop-chop!

You're trying to back out of a tight spot between two cars in the supermarket parking lot. *Scrr-r-rrape!* You hear your bumper rub against the front fender of the car to your right. But you keep going and have just pulled into the clear when suddenly the owner of that car comes running up, spots his dented fender and yells, "Hey, did you just bang my fender!"

Dramatize your denial by switching gears, literally and figuratively. Immediately go into forward speed, as though you were pulling *in*, and yell: "How could I have banged your fender when I haven't even parked yet!"

Just don't hit him again.

It's parents' visiting day at grade school and, being a good father, you attend. You watch the class in session, enjoying it very much especially when the teacher declares that your son wrote the best composition in class and calls upon him to read it aloud. But to your great astonishment—and humiliation—junior pipes up, "Hey, daddy, that's the one *you* wrote for me!"

You need a Lightning Lie. Correct him at once: "*Typed*, not wrote!" Then immediately, in an exasperated whisper, turn to the teacher and say, "I typed it out for him because he'd hurt his hand in a stickball game and couldn't hold a pen."

Fear can be a great motivator of ingenious alibis. Here you are driving along on one of those narrow country roads and the road hog creeping along in front of you won't let you pass. You toot and toot without ever taking your hand off the horn. Suddenly, the road hog sticks his hand out and stops short, causing you to jam on your brakes. You are madder than ever and intend to give this guy hell—until you see what comes out of the car. This guy is Gargantua himself, fists clenched, blood in his eye, and clearly on the way to tear you to pieces.

Are you doomed? No, but you're too scared to be angry any more. Just change your tune and yell out: "Boy, am I glad I finally got your attention, mister. Your rear wheels are wobbling like crazy and I was worried that you'd wind up in a ditch!"

He'll be so stunned by this unexpected explanation that he'll thank you and wave you on to pass him while he inches his way to the nearest gas station—by which time you should have put at least 50 miles between you.

You had a big night and slept right through the early

morning sales meeting. You know you're going to catch it from the sales manager. To avoid a showdown, you need to prepare a classic cop-out in advance.

Before making your entrance, open your shirt, crumple your tie, tear the buttons off your jacket and muss your hair. Then barge into the sales manager's office, and pant, "Well, I made it, chief. You'll probably see me on tonight's TV newscast."

The manager will be taken completely off stride. Dumbfounded, he'll exclaim, "What the hell are you talking about? What happened to you? Why weren't you at the meeting?"

Tell him ruefully, "I guess you haven't heard. There was a demonstration* going on downtown and I got caught in it. They almost tore me apart. I never thought I'd make it here alive."

Your secret vice is *pot*, but you're very nervous about buying it from anyone. So you decide to grow your own. You plant your *cannabis sativa* in your backyard garden, camouflaging the stuff by planting ordinary vegetables around it. But when the plants begin to bloom and show their leaves, some snoopy neighbors start to eye your vegetable patch suspiciously. If you try to get away with

---

* There's always a demonstration going on somewhere. Here's a sample list of popular demos for future reference: Gay Liberation, NOW, Women's Strike for Peace, Mobilization for Youth, and the three big catch-alls—Civil Rights, Anti-War, and Student Protest demos.

simply telling them it's a tomato plant, they'll never believe you.

How do you fake them out?

Purchase a bunch of very small, very green tomatoes and drop them on the soil. When your neighbors come snooping around, point proudly to the green fruit and say proudly: "Well, my tomato plants are really thriving."

The sight of real tomatoes will throw them off the track.

The next time you're stopped for jaywalking or for smoking in the subway or when attempting to crash the long line at the movies, the bus stop, or the supermarket:

Try this lie-lapalooza. All you have to do is memorize this line: *"Yah nee pony mah'yoo."** Deliver it with a puzzled look on your face. Whoever is bothering you will think you're a foreigner, shrug his shoulders and give up.

We call this being alibilingual.

The "impossible" alibi

And now that you've read this book, has it sharpened your alibi I.Q.? Think you can lie like a trouper? Then test yourself on this inextricable situation, which only an ultra-alibi artist can crack:

* Russian (spelled phonetically) for: "I do not understand."

It's Sunday morning, and you're having sex with your wife. Suddenly your little kid, who *never* gets up this early, walks in on you! How do you handle the situation? Give up?

Here's your "impossible" alibi: "Sonny, wait outside until Daddy and Mommy finish our exercise."

That's known as making your bed and lieing in it.

And it should satisfy Dr. Freud, Dr. Spock, and Dr. Reuben.

Our final alibi

As a closing tribute to ourselves, we offer this epitaph—to be engraved, not in granite, but out of respect for alibi traditions, in plastic or some other reasonable facsimile:

"Here lie Mort Weisinger and Art Henley—
as usual."